Mike Hill

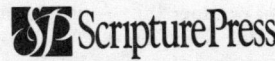

Amersham-on-the-Hill, Bucks HP6 6JQ, England

© 1994 by Mike Hill

All rights reserved. No part of this book may be reproduced
in any form without permission in writing from the publisher,
except in the case of brief quotations embodied in critical
articles or reviews.

ISBN 1 898938 00 8

Designed and produced for Alpha, an imprint of
SCRIPTURE PRESS FOUNDATION (UK) LTD
Raans Road, Amersham-on-the-Hill, Bucks HP6 6JQ,
England by Nuprint Ltd, Harpenden, Herts AL5 4SE.

Contents

Foreword 9

1 Mission Beyond the Church Fringe 11
2 Introducing Willow Creek 25
3 Who are the Seekers? 41
4 Starting the Process 53
5 The Congregation in 'Mission Mode' 75
6 The Seeker Service 97
7 Re-ordering the Church for Mission 127
8 Small Beginnings 139

Appendix I 151
  How can we become more seeker sensitive?

Appendix II 153
  Questionnaire

DEDICATION

For the people of St. Leonard's Church,
Chesham Bois,
who taught me more than they will ever know.

Foreword

Mike Hill's heart beats for irreligious people. He has a passionate desire to see the local church successfully penetrate British culture with the powerful truth of the Gospel. This thought-provoking and insightful book is yet another step in his quest to see ministries become more strategic in reaching the unchurched with the life-changing message of Jesus Christ.

My association with Mike began when he played an instrumental role in bringing a team from Willow Creek Community Church to participate in a conference in Birmingham, England, in June 1992. I'll never forget how the Holy Spirit energized and guided that exciting gathering as pastors from around the UK discussed ideas for building churches that would increasingly reach the unchurched.

During the last several years, Mike has visited Willow Creek's campus and our Church Leadership Conferences several times. He is knowledgeable about the values that undergird our efforts to reach the 'Unchurched Harry's and Mary's' of Chicago, and I'm very pleased that he has written this book to discuss these core beliefs from a British perspective.

Some of the strategy that God has led us to employ at Willow Creek may be transferable to the British context; some might not be. That's for British leaders to discern. And I'm glad that Mike has offered this book as a way to further that discussion.

It's my hope that the end result will be great advances for God's Kingdom as this 'Decade of Evangelism' continues to unfold.

Bill Hybels
South Barrington, Ill. USA
March, 1994

1

Mission Beyond the Church Fringe

'It's not the Church of God which has a mission, it's the God of Mission who has a Church.' Those words I attribute to Dr Tim Dearborne who at that time was teaching theology at Aberdeen University. The context of his remark was the great Inter-Varsity Student Missions Conference held every three years in the USA. He was delivering the daily Bible reading to the pastors attending the conference.

Somehow that particular remark stuck with me. I can remember thinking at the time that its thrust was significant. What is being said? Firstly, that God is a sending God. Our word 'mission' comes from the Latin *missio*, which means, 'I send'. God **sends** His Son into the world (John 3:16); He **sends** His Spirit to His Church (Acts 2:4) and He **sends** His Church to make disciples of all the nations (Matthew 28:19). He is in this sense a missionary God. God is sending Himself into the world.

Secondly, the quote implies that God looks for His people, the Church, to join Him in that missionary task. As mission lies within the heart of God so we are called to be a missionary people. It was Emil Brunner who wrote that the Church exists by mission as a fire exists by burning. It is an uncomfortable thought. For how many of our churches would imply by their behaviour that mission was their purpose in life, their *raison d'etre*?

It is undoubtedly true that most churches have a self-image which they describe as 'friendly'. Without exception, at the many church conferences and weekends that I have been involved with, the churches concerned have always listed 'friendliness' as a strength. What is equally clear is that such a self perception is not how they are viewed from the outside. Many who give the local church a try find them far from friendly. Ministers are only too well aware that at the now mandatory 'coffee after the service', newcomers are left to stand awkwardly on their own whilst the faithful chat away in their own groups. The perception of friendliness within church fellowships communicates itself as something different to those who try and join.

Of course it's not just the people who send signals about the 'user-friendliness' of our churches.

Church members themselves have become disillusioned: hence the decline in traditional churches and the growth of house churches and religious communities. To some extent the whole of what we do communicates what we are about. Body language relates to churches as much as individuals! It issues from a mindset and this is largely what this book is about. God shows no partiality: nor should we to those attending our churches.

Missions and Mission

Undoubtedly the Decade of Evangelism has had a positive impact. Some churches who previously would have found it difficult to put evangelism on the agenda are waking up to the fact that seeking and saving the lost is OK. Church planting is also a viable strategy which many churches are finding effective. Conferences on evangelism abound and local missions frequently involving churches working together are being planned or have already taken place. There is much to thank God for. However, for all the flurry of activity, there still lurks a basic question.

> **Does the activity engendered by the Decade represent a basic change in the mind-set of the British Church from self-maintenance to mission?**

Bishop Nigel McCulloch, Chairman of the Decade Steering Group, wrote in a recent article after noting some of the positive aspects of the Decade thus far, 'It has to be said, sadly, that some of the responses to the Decade call have been so superficial, both in intention and application, as to be an insult to God whose mission we are meant to be about.'[1] Plain speaking indeed!

What did the Bishop mean by this? Clearly he recognises that something is not right. His article, admittedly slanted fairly directly at the Anglican Church, speaks about the need for repentance in our churches. A repentance based upon our willingness to admit to God that we have been travelling in a wrong direction and expressing a fervent desire to ask for His Guidance for **His** Mission. My guess is that such a sentiment has relevance for all the Churches of our land.

The more I see the Decade unfold, the more I realise that evangelism will succeed only when the whole people of God are involved. But this is being obscured by our pre-occupation with the 'crusade mission' concept of evangelism. Such crusades, which have served us well in the past, seem to be the main tool for the present. In a good many areas the question of 'What to do?' is answered by 'More of the same'. Special missions can become a substitute for the true mission of the Church.

Mission Strategy

Recently I was asked to attend a mission. Large sums of money had been invested in a large and comfortable tent. The atmosphere was informal and relaxed; the musician and singer for the evening were adequate though the lyrics were not particularly appropriate for a missionary context. The speaker, a well-known and very gifted evangelist, gave an excellent message addressing the issue of human suffering.

At the end the appeal to make 'a decision for Christ' was made. From a crowd of six to seven hundred people about six people came forward to be prayed with. I am well aware that there is great joy in heaven when one sinner repents and I thank God for the evangelistic gifts of the speaker on that occasion and those whose lives were touched. However, I came away with some questions about crusade mission as the main strategy for mission.

Recently a commissioning editor from a Christian publishing company approached me and asked if I could think of anyone who could start 'far enough back' in writing material for the unchurched. She had searched the Christian market place for such a talent without success. Through my mind went the names of many of the gifted Christian communicators I know. Reluctantly, I had to admit that I couldn't think of anyone who was up to the task, though part of me would have loved to volunteer myself, I recognise that I couldn't fit the bill either.

Part of my worry with the crusade mission strategy is the way in which the main events are not set up 'far enough back' for the unchurched of our land. It's difficult to preach a traditional gospel message in such a way that many of the unchurched people will understand what we're talking about. Realities which are familiar currency to those of us who have been brought up on them are a long way from where a lot of people today are starting out.

In saying this I am not saying that the traditional gospel is somehow defective and that sophisticated modern humanity cannot believe old-fashioned Gospel truths. On the contrary, I would wish to argue very strongly that the message of the Gospel as we have received it in Scripture is the only answer to the human predicament. What I am saying, though, is that we need to incarnate that wonderful message in ways that the unchurched people will be able to get hold of it, see its relevance and respond.

The Strengths of the Crusade Mission Model

I don't believe that the crusade mission strategy is dead or irrelevant. I do believe that it is a seriously limited option and that we still rely far too heavily on it. It does however have some obvious strengths.

It creates an environment which is usually not dominated by church buildings. Mostly events take place in neutral venues such as football grounds or people's homes or even public houses. To this extent it is 'user-friendly'. This is surely a step in the right direction. Though many British Christians seem obsessed by the symbolic value of church buildings it is difficult to see any value unchurched people place upon them other than as a backdrop for the photographs at family occasions or as part of our heritage to be preserved at all cost!

Another strength of the crusade mission is that it provides a positive route to commitment – unlike many church services. People are given an opportunity to make a decision. The way that a decision can be actioned is clearly explained and those who wish to proceed are encouraged to do so. In my experience the charge that such occasions are 'psychological manipulation' or 'emotional hype' have little basis in reality. I remember when attending my first crusade feeling a little cheated that it was so unemotional!

Crusade mission will continue to play an important role in bringing people to Christ, particularly with those who have lapsed in their Christian commitment or perhaps in days past had a positive experience of a Christian Church, including those who already attend church. Occasionally, people will be converted who have had no experience of the Christian Church and for all the people who have and will come into the Church this way, I thank God. There is little doubt that the ministry of Billy Graham, Luis Palau, J. John and others has profoundly shaped the Christian landscape around the world.

The Weaknesses of the Crusade Mission Model

I don't want to be heard to be over-critical of the crusade model. However, the following comments are some worries that I have.

I suppose my first anxiety is the drop-out rate. Jesus gave the Church a Commission to 'make disciples'. I take it that every evangelist sets the target of preparing the way for people to become fully devoted followers of Jesus Christ. Preparation for follow-up after the mission is always high on the agenda before the mission, but getting people from the excitement of a decision made at a large crusade in a football ground into church membership is not straightforward. Many drop out between the two venues. To those who think they've found 'it' at a Crusade, arrival at the local church can often be a shock. For despite the follow-up seminars run before the crusade many churches are just not geared to receiving new Christians. In many cases it's a bit like taking a new born baby and dumping it at a museum rather than nurturing it in the post-natal ward!

My second area of reservation relates to the rather complacent attitude that such evangelism can breed in Christians. To call in the expert, go through all the preparation, attend the event (in most cases without taking an unchurched friend) and put some money in the hat is to make us feel we've done it! That's it for a few years till the minister challenges us again to take on a missionary project. If the aim of a crusade is to see people won for Christ and become His fully devoted followers it is unlikely that one brief and concerted effort is going to prove highly effective. A crusade mission is much more likely to be effective in the context of an ongoing programme of mission of which the crusade is but a part. The truth is that quite a number of missions don't bring in many new people and so churches justify their worthy endeavours by speaking of 'the blessing it brought to the local church'!

I suspect there's a more subtle edge to the attraction of the crusade. Because it takes place beyond the local church it allows us to maintain our churches as we like them and have grown to love them whilst making us feel that we've done our bit for those who don't come.

The key question that many churches refuse to face in preparation for their mission is:

> **'What kind of church will we need to become to receive and to nurture spiritual babies?'**

I recently posed this question to a friend who has been the driving force behind a large city crusade mission. With great sadness of heart he looked me in the eye and said, 'That's what really bothers me'.

Well, that's what really bothers me as well. Of course, you can't lay the blame for maintenance-minded churches at the feet of our crusade evangelists. You could however argue that evangelistic strategies which attempt to avoid the need for our churches to change, will have limited impact. The further that our nation moves away from God the more limited the appeal of these strategies will become.

Some crusade leaders now advocate that new converts should be nurtured for a few weeks in a home environment before inviting them to church: quite literally the church is the last place to invite them to. It seems strange when we have to protect people from our churches.

The Culture Gap

The issue of the Gospel and culture is a huge issue about which much has been written many times in recent years. Needless to say that an understanding of the relationship between the two is crucial in the formation of a viable strategy for mission and follow-up. That relationship is not an easy one for at its heart there lies a paradox. It is that the Gospel needs to reside within a culture whilst at the same time that same Gospel will, if obeyed, ask some uncomfortable questions of that culture. The balance is delicate and probably one that no individual community of Christians gets right.

To ignore the culture in which the Gospel resides risks the Church becoming a counter sub-culture. A classic example of this is certain aspects of the 19th century missionary movement. The existence of English church architecture in the middle of Eastern cities; local peoples being taught to sing Wesley's hymns and 'dress up' for Church services are the harvest of ignoring the local culture. Thankfully, I don't think that many Christians would be happy with such a culturally imperialistic approach to mission today, but there are many conflicts of cultures within our own neighbourhoods.

To reside in a culture without being prepared to ask some of the awkward questions that the Gospel demands seems to be well illustrated by the church in this country today, particularly in middle class suburbia. In such contexts the local culture seems almost too easily assimilated by the church. The church lives readily in that culture but rarely challenges any of its core values. The resulting distortion of the Christian faith is a form of Christianity which will be quick to judge certain kinds of immorality, often trivial such as bad language on the television—but never even questions the morality of encouraging the spending of thousands of pounds on material goods or the portrayal of unbiblical ethics.

Beyond the Fringe

The reason for raising the vast issue of the Gospel and culture at this stage is that I fear that, as a Church, we have targeted only the 'fringe' around our church life. Most of our strategies when you analyse them are far more likely to be effective with that group: crusade missions, baptism preparation, pastoral contact, guest services, pram services, etc, etc. Of course it's perfectly possible to build a healthy local church on such strategies and don't let me stop you!

This book is an attempt to try and start a process which will get you to look 'beyond the fringe' to the 80-plus per cent of people in Britain who know very little about the Christian faith and are unlikely to come to a church service without some good reason. These are the people who, when they do come to many of our churches as they are, are left bored and bewildered by what they confront. For many of them the issue of their culture and the culture of the Church is one that we will need to do some serious thinking about.

As I read the Bible I see the story of a God who is

interested in lost people. His Son Jesus reflects that concern by telling stories about lost coins and lost sheep and a lost son (Luke 15). He tells us that the Son of Man came to seek and to save the lost. I can't resist the feeling that because lost people were so high on the Divine Agenda they should be high on the agenda of His Church today.

There are plenty of Christians who go about lamenting the state of the world in which we live. They are good on diagnosis; they know only too well the prognosis. They have personal experience of the cure, but they're not willing to get involved in sharing that cure with a dying world. What will it take for us to get involved?

The Need to Change

The reality of a changing world brings with it the uncomfortable thought that we, the Church, might have to change.

> **We have to find ways of providing churches for the growing numbers of the unchurched even at the risk of alienating the faithful.**

After all it was Jesus that taught, in the parable of the lost sheep (Luke 15:3-7), that the shepherd was prepared to put the well-being of the ninety-nine sheep at risk in order to seek after his one lost sheep.

'Going to Church' has had times of popularity and appeal. For example, at the dawn of the 19th century, England saw phenomenal growth in the nonconformist churches. Starting off amongst working class people, the impact of their message became effective amongst the emerging middle classes and larger and larger churches and chapels were built. Today's isolation of the church had begun by the end of the last century whilst attendance was still high and the culture strong without an apparent need to change in a rapidly changing world. But the pub was reinforcing its position as the haven for the masses rather than the book-orientated worship and meeting places of Victorian Protestantism. They were unwilling to change their culture without seeming to lose the very values that had made the churches and chapels so successful in the first place.

The decline of church attendance early in the 20th century was apparent for all to see. It was a decline that affected virtually all Protestant churches but impacted nonconformist churches more than any other segment of church life. Within two decades powerful, vibrant, self-confident nonconformity had become something of a relic. It would be difficult not to argue that today, for many people, the Church as a whole is seen as an irrelevant and out of date institution with little to offer.

It seems likely, however, that the pillars of scientific rationalism and philosophical materialism upon which our modern culture is founded are crumbling. Modern humanity seems to have discovered the fundamental biblical truth that man cannot live on bread alone. Disturbing is the fact that a resurgence of interest in 'things spiritual' does not seem to herald a massive swing back to the Christian faith. The beneficiaries of this disillusionment with material and rationalist values seem to be the fringe spiritualities, broadly lumped under the umbrella term 'New Age'.

If, as Christians, we believe the gospel to be true, there rightly will be little enthusiasm for altering our

Mission Beyond the Church Fringe 23

message. True, some churches have found a measure of growth through worldliness, seeking popularity in being all things to all people whilst compromising faith and doctrine. Such a compromise is dangerous.

> **The real question is how can we create churches which are uncompromising in love, faith and doctrine but are relevant to the age we live in?**

2

Introducing Willow Creek

'Why should anybody seriously think that a church ministering in suburban Chicago would have anything to offer the UK Church scene? After all it's American.'

Such a response or something similar will be on the lips or in the minds of many Christians outside America. To tell the truth it was in my mind. Then I arrived at Willow Creek Community Church. At the age of 41 I stood on the frost scorched earth looking across the lake at Willow Creek with a lump in my throat. I had just attended one of their services. For the first time in my life I had experienced a kind of church that articulated for me everything I had always believed the Church should be. It was a powerful moment.

I left Chicago a few days later and flew back to the UK. What was it that had so impressed me with the place? Was it the building? Modern, plush and extremely well maintained, the building at Willow Creek is larger than an English Cathedral with a recent extension the size of an airport terminal. The site is 127 acres with car parking facilities that would make the same facilities at a UK superstore look limited. A Christian from outside the USA cannot help be awestruck by the physical scale of Willow Creek, especially a UK Christian.

Could it Happen Elsewhere?

Impressive though the buildings are, I can truthfully say that I didn't come back to the UK with a burning desire to get on with a building project. I would like to think of myself as something of a realist and I had worked it out that to buy one acre of building land with planning permission would be something of a tall order for even some of the larger UK churches. Though I've learnt over the years that the environment in which we meet, to work or to worship, to study or to pray, is very important, it wasn't the building that captured my imagination.

Was it the large congregation packed into the 4,500-seater auditorium? I have to confess that part of the clutter of my British ecclesiastical heritage is the uneasy feeling that when large numbers of people are showing up for religion there's something unhealthy going on. My warning antennae are immediately switched on. However, I can't pretend, as I watched the traffic police try to sort out the traffic congestion on the approaches to Willow Creek, that I didn't long to see people in the UK having to queue to get into church.

On the whole I don't really believe in the megachurch concept. Having been a Minister at what in UK terms is a large local church I'm not convinced. It seems to me that congregations with membership around the 180-200 mark make the best sense. Such churches will have enough people to implement effective ministry strategies. They will also retain for individual members a real sense of belonging. Congregations of this size also make more sense pastorally.

For many Ministers the idea of a large congregation will be a seductive attraction. The reasons for that are largely obvious. But add to these the fact that the large church is a pretty rare phenomenon in the UK and so most Ministers do not have any experience of the pressures and problems of leadership in a larger context so it's easy to see how the size thing can be a powerful demotivator. My hunch is that the 'mega church', if it ever happens in the UK, will be rare—and that may not be a bad thing.

Leadership Requirements

Was it the dynamic leadership and remarkable communication gifts of Senior Pastor, Bill Hybels? Well, if you think that good leadership is crucial, then you can't easily remove Hybels from the Willow Creek equation. He is without doubt a visionary.

> **I don't claim to know him well, but everything I've seen of Bill points to a man who is humble in spirit, who walks with God and is effective in mobilising his membership to trust God and to live as though they do.**

His great sense of humour is matched by a willingness to be disarmingly honest about his personal life. As a speaker he is literally 'phenomenal'. Many of the 1,600 church leaders who gathered at the International Conference Centre in Birmingham in June 1992 for the first UK Church Leader's Conference were both moved and inspired by Bill's giftedness as a speaker. A senior church leader confessed to me after the conference, 'I knew he had something to teach me. What I didn't expect was to be ministered to at such depth through his speaking ministry.' It's this aspect of Bill's ministry that makes those who want to categorise him as one of the new breed of entrepreneurial church leaders a little hasty in their judgements. He is not a 'machine' church leader who relies solely on the insights of business management, psychology and marketing to achieve his goals. He shows a huge reliance upon the Holy Spirit and the authority of the Bible. It is doubtful whether someone who didn't show such reliance would touch the lives of seasoned Christian campaigners in such a way.

His leadership and vision is clearly very important to the way that Willow Creek has developed. The Church claims to exist for a four-fold purpose. The aspects of this four-fold purpose are not in essence different than many churches would claim for their mission statement. Indeed, they are hardly revolutionary. Their purpose is described in the following way:

Exaltation: Willow Creek exists to offer the fellowship of believers the opportunity to worship and glorify God together.

Edification: Willow Creek exists to assist believers to build a foundation of biblical understanding, develop a devotional life, discover their spiritual gifts and to encourage believers to become participants in the life of the Church.

Evangelism: Willow Creek exists to reach people who do not have a Christian faith. Members of the Church are encouraged to seek out the unchurched as the Holy Spirit has sought them out, and to look for opportunities to share Christ's love.

Social Action: Willow Creek exists to act as a conscience to the world by demonstrating the love and righteousness of God in both word and deed.

The Concept of 'Church'

This four-fold purpose is achieved by what, at Willow Creek, is known as the seven-step philosophy. Before considering that, however, there is an important emphasis in the teaching of Willow Creek that is worthy of close scrutiny. Without exception, when I have heard Bill Hybels teach the seven-step philosophy he has started by declaring his passion for the Church.

Part of Hybel's training for ministry involved sitting at the feet of Dr Gilbert Bilezikian, a remarkable teacher of theology, who today still teaches at Wheaton College, Illinois. Hybels regularly and genuinely expresses his gratitude to 'Dr B' for his help and theological input. To some extent, Dr Bilezikian has acted as a theological consultant to Willow Creek over the years and is still very much in evidence today. He has regularly participated in the weekend Seeker's Services.

One of the strong influences that Dr Bilezikian had on Hybels was to emphasise the importance of the Church in God's plan for the redemption of the world. This teaching had a strong impact on Bill Hybels.

In speaking about one of the common theological perceptions that was shared by the small group of young Christians that founded Willow Creek, Hybels says, 'God drew together a small band of people who really believed that the greatest thing going in all the world was the Church.'

The reason I mention this is that it seems to me to be a foundation that underpins the whole Willow Creek strategy. It is significant, as a common criticism of Evangelical Christianity that it has given little attention to a theology of the church. Maybe history will show that one of the contributions that Willow Creek will make to the wider church, not least the evangelicals, will be a restored love of the Church as the Body of Christ here on earth.

Willow Creek is one of the many Independent Churches in the USA. It is by tradition a Protestant, inter-denominational, evangelical Bible-believing church which believes in exalting God, edifying believers, evangelising the unchurched and demonstrating love through social action. As Hybels jokes, when you tell people what kind of church Willow Creek is in such terms, 'it'll knock their socks off!'

The Seven-step Philosophy

Step 1. It's the responsibility of every church member to build relationships with unchurched people

Willow Creek bases its evangelism strategy on a relational or friendship evangelism basis. One aspect of the core teaching of Willow Creek that emerges time and time again is the message that 'lost people matter to God'. This first step is crucial. Without it the whole strategy falls down. Hybels teaches consistently from texts such as Luke 15, illustrating God's concern for lost people. In the parable of the lost sheep the well-being of the ninety-nine sheep is put in jeopardy whilst the shepherd goes in search of the lost one. The parable ends with a reminder about the heavenly celebration which ensues when one sinner is saved. This teaching, put alongside the Great Commission in Matthew 28, provides a firm, biblical basis for the Church to share in God's concern for lost people.

The difficulty for many Christians is that they become taken over by a church culture. Because so many churches have such a strong activity base, much time is taken up responding (or feeling guilty for not responding), to the weekly prompt in the church notices that 'all are welcome' to all or most of those activities. In consequence many Christians quite quickly lose contact with their non-Christian friends largely because their local church takes them over. There simply isn't the time.

Perhaps it's time for many churches to re-assess what they are doing in this respect. It's confusing for many Christians to be exhorted during the teaching time to create relationships with their non-Christian friends whilst at the same time being encouraged during the notices to spend large amounts of their leisure time supporting church events.

> **It may well be that if we are to become serious about evangelism, one of our starting points will be a review of our church activities in order to give time to our church members to develop relationships with non-Christians.**

Most Christians recognise the fact that the best basis for evangelism is friendship. In a way it's obvious, for most of us don't accept new things from people we don't know. When someone steps out of the crowd in the street to try and speak to us about transcendental meditation or the plight of refugees in a far-off country most of us are immediately on the defensive. Our personal space is being invaded and we don't like it. Part of this is because we don't know the person making the offer. The context of a relationship makes the whole thing a lot safer—even if ultimately we aren't that interested in what our friend is talking about. A friendship implies a framework of trust which is significant when important truths are to be communicated.

In consequence, every believer attending Willow Creek Community Church is exhorted to build relationships of integrity with their non-Christian friends—constantly referred to as 'unchurched Harry and Mary' by Bill Hybels. 'Unchurched Harry and Mary' are largely untouched by traditional churches. They probably have very little knowledge of the Christian faith and more significantly, very little recognisable desire to learn anything about it. Their view of Church will be fashioned by TV caricatures and stories of wayward clergy in the Press. For most of these people the only real possibility of having that mind-set challenged will come through a relationship of integrity with a believer.

Step 2. It's the privilege of each believer to share a verbal witness as the opportunity arises

Many preachers have exhorted their flocks to share a verbal witness as the Spirit prompts them. In Acts 1:8 Jesus tells his disciples that their task is to be witnesses. Clearly those early disciples were witnesses to the

Resurrection of Christ. Today a primary task of disciples is to witness to the risen life of Jesus.

The early Church understood Jesus to be handing them a mandate to take the Good News of the risen Christ out into the known world – though, as the early verses of Acts 8 tell us, it took a violent persecution to energise that mandate. It seems that the reluctance many Christians have to witness to their faith has been around for a very long time. However, without the willingness of Christians to share a verbal witness, the mission of the Church is seriously hindered. A key question for any church gearing itself for serious outreach is, 'What will it take for the Christians in this place to speak to their non-Christian friends about their faith?'

In some ways the answers to such a question are predictable. The need for training in how to present a word of testimony is vital. The need for that fundamental Christian characteristic, courage, is usually identified twinned with sensitivity to know the right place and time to share a testimony in love (1 Peter 3:15). None of these issues are insurmountable and yet so many Christians have ruled out the idea of ever speaking about their Christian faith lest they be thought to be fanatics or their witness is rejected, or even worse mocked.

Willow Creek stresses the vital importance of Christians being willing and prepared to share a verbal witness as the opportunity arises. Training is given on how and when to present a word of personal testimony. Certainly at Willow Creek there seems to be a recognition of the truth first recognised by the authorities in Jerusalem that if you want to stop the Church from spreading the best thing to do is to stop it from speaking (Acts 4:18). Again, this second step is vital to the evangelism strategy of Willow Creek. Without this principle the whole seven-step philosophy is rendered impotent.

At this stage it is worth pointing out an important cultural difference between the USA and the UK. In the USA where a majority of people still claim to be 'born again' Christians, the spiritual climate feels somewhat different. In such a context it is arguably more acceptable to own publicly a Christian belief. Because of this, it is observed, the idea of speaking about Christianity does not seem as daunting to believers in the USA as it does to believers in the UK. Certainly this is not an insignificant factor. In consequence if we are to see churches grow outside the North American scene we shall need a real investment of time and training in this matter of enabling people to share a verbal witness. I certainly believe that churches which are able to energise and motivate their congregations in this way will be the growth churches of the future.

One cultural fantasy we Christians commonly hold in the UK is that there are three subjects to be avoided in everyday conversation—sex, politics and religion. Such a fantasy adds to our nervousness about saying anything about our personal beliefs. The reason I label this perception a fantasy is that several years of life in commerce and many hours sitting in public houses (before I was a Christian of course!) led me to see that the main topics of conversation (plus sport) were sex, politics and religion! Maybe the whole thing is safer than we think. A problem we have in this is that we have lost the art of speaking naturally about our faith. Somehow it always seems so forced.

Step 3. Providing a service for seekers

It is true that a fairly typical response to a positive experience of a verbal witness or a response at a mission or crusade is a desire to know more. Even those who are 'soundly converted' at such events have little knowledge of what is expected of believers in terms of behaviour and beliefs. A well-used and very viable strategy in many churches is the nurture or enquirer's group which, in a small group context, explores the fundamentals of the Christian faith. Many churches have used these groups to great effect. However, there are some limitations.

Firstly, a small group context can be a very threatening environment for some people. Shyness, a fear of being made to look silly or ignorant and the behaviour of difficult people are all amplified in a small group context. Secondly, the small group keeps people away from the church's worship. Basis to Willow Creek's theology is that when it comes to the development of fully-devoted followers of Jesus Christ, it is a mistake to avoid the issue of Church. Willow Creek attempts to address this by providing services which are as accessible as possible to seekers. Indeed, these services are designed especially for seekers and introduce them to the church as an important first step in the discipling process. It is surely a very sad reflection on the curious, inward-looking replica of the Church that prevails today that we have to devise 'follow-up' strategies after big missions which postpone for as long as possible introducing new believers to the Church's worship.

The Willow Creek Church Leaders' Handbook states, 'The services are designed for people who are in the process of making a decision for Christ or evaluating

Christianity, and for those who have recently committed their lives to Him.' These services at present take place three times over the weekend at Willow Creek, on Saturday evening and on Sundays at 9.30 am and 11 am. The decision on timing was not an arbitrary decision. Careful, local research indicated that Sunday morning within their culture was the best time for such a service. The addition of Saturday evening was the result of a later decision. The content and detail of these services will be dealt with later, but the Seeker Service is a brilliant and highly-developed strategy in the Willow Creek plan.

Step 4. Attending the New Community Service

'New Community' is the name Willow Creek has given to its weekly services for believers. There is a built-in assumption that if people were to attend only the Seeker Services their spiritual diet would be somewhat imbalanced. This service provides Willow Creek believers with an opportunity to participate in worship and to be fed with more expository preaching than would happen in the Seeker Service. The aim of this service is to assist the believer grow to maturity and to allow for a fuller expression of worship than would be deemed appropriate in the Seeker Service.

Strong exhortations are given 'from the top' to attend New Community services, which happen on Wednesday and Thursday evenings at 7.30 pm. Thursday evening is an exact repeat of the Wednesday programme. Once a month the New Community evening event is a celebration of the Lord's Supper.

Though it would be expected that attendance at the New Community nights would be less than weekend attendance at the Seeker Services, there is a feeling that the New Community nights don't command the priority amongst Willow Creek believers that they might. I suspect, and the attendance figures would support the fact, that quite a number of believers only attend Seeker Services.

Step 5. Participation in a small group

The next step in the process of discipleship is the encouragement to participate in a small group. As the Willow Creek Handbook puts it, 'Small group involvement provides fellowship for the believer as well as a group for accountability, discipleship, encouragement and support.'

Ideally, small groups should consist of 8–10 people who meet for a weekly period of two years. The Church has a special department which caters for a curriculum of study to develop discipleship within the small group. Again, the importance of membership of a small group is repeatedly stressed at Willow Creek, but not in isolation from the main meetings.

Step 6. Involvement in service

Those who become members of Willow Creek are challenged, as part of the process of membership, to identify their spiritual gift(s) and to offer them in the service of Christ and for the edification of His Church. Recognising that people often find it difficult to locate their spiritual giftedness, help is at hand to assist Church members in the process. Christian leadership at the church and small group participation can help people identify and utilise their spiritual gifts. It is taught by the teaching team at Willow Creek that Christians who do not exercise their spiritual gift(s) are usually frustrated in their Christian discipleship. Certainly they will not reach their spiritual potential.

Step 7. Christian Stewardship

In Willow Creek language, the term 'stewardship' relates to the area of money management and the serious consideration of how God can be honoured through personal giving. It is worth stating that Willow Creek is not the stereotype of the way a lot of British people conceive of the Church in the USA. It is not obsessed by money nor does it create elaborate and theatrical ways of extracting money from attenders. Indeed at the Sunday Seeker Service it is strongly stressed, 'The offering is for members of this Church. If you are a visitor please don't participate.'

However there is an appreciation of a basic fact in today's society. Ministry costs money. A full-time staff of about 150 people, with another 125 part-time staff, a large church complex to maintain, and many social programmes to sponsor demand a sound donor base. Members of the church, as part of the process of membership, are challenged to think about their financial commitment to the church. Teaching is given regularly on proper stewardship. The dangers of debt, a covetous spirit, learning to be gracious with possessions, and sharing with those who are in need, all form part of the stewardship programme. The results are impressive. To enter into membership at Willow Creek implies a financial commitment to the church.

Clearly the aim of this seven-step philosophy is to transform unchurched people into fully-devoted followers of Jesus Christ. In the suburban Chicago context it has proved to be a very fruitful strategy. A very key question is, whether or not this strategy has

Introducing Willow Creek 39

application elsewhere? Certainly Willow Creek do not claim that this is a strategy designed to give universal success.

Portraying God's Concern for People

Yet as a strategy, the seven-step Philosophy has a lot going for it. It begins with a very fundamental principle which is very different than in most churches. Right at the heart of Willow Creek's 'genetic make-up' is a built-in DNA-type code about God's passion for lost people. In most churches such a belief is either not evident or marginalised. That's one reason for the common perception amongst many unchurched people that the Church is a rather eccentric club with its own agenda and rules. Most churches send very few signals about their concern (and, in consequence, God's concern) for those who never warm their pews. At Willow Creek it's different. Its very reason for existence is God's concern for the lost. Some would argue, myself included, that such a foundational belief is entirely justifiable and indeed a lot closer to the early Church than much of what we experience today in most churches. In a post-Christian context it is vital to the survival of the Church.

> **A key question is how can we address the issue of changing the mind-set of the contemporary church to become truly mission minded?**

3

Who are the Seekers?

Thinking about it, I realise that having made several visits to Willow Creek, and heard the seven-step philosophy explained on numerous occasions, I have never yet actually heard anyone attempt to define exactly what a 'seeker' is. Considering that the seeker is the target of much of what Willow Creek is about, it seems somewhat strange that no one seems over-occupied with a working definition.

The New Testament seems vaguely encouraging in this area, but again doesn't attempt any direct definition. Jesus encouraged people to 'seek and you will find'. People like Nicodemus and Zacchaeus came to Christ with an apparent interest in wanting to know more about Him. Obviously, during Jesus' life and ministry here on earth it was somehow easier to 'seek' him because of His physical presence. Almost 2,000 years of human history has elapsed since then. What does it mean to be a seeker today?

Are there any characteristics that will help us delineate who is a seeker and who is not? Perhaps we could

42 *Reaching the Unchurched*

safely assume that because God made us with a spiritual aspect to our nature—which can only be fulfilled by faith in Him—that all people are in some sense seekers? Such a belief will mean that some of the dominant features of secular society, such as materialism, are merely futile attempts at trying to find fulfilment in life without God. When Jesus said, 'You can't serve God and Mammon' he seemed to be implying that 'Mammon' was a rival God. There is some appeal in such a theory. God is concerned for all people and I believe He calls His Church to share that concern. The idea that all people are seekers reinforces the view that the Christian community should never give up on anyone.

I do however, see some difficulties with this thinking. Firstly, that it does ignore a slightly difficult strand of biblical teaching. When Jesus sent out the 72 he told them not to waste too much time on those who did not give them a welcome. In fact they were to make a symbolic gesture in leaving a home where they did not receive a welcome. As the old evangelists used to teach, 'Evangelism is about picking ripe apples rather than tugging at green ones.' Jesus' saying that the 'harvest is plentiful, but the labourers are few' strengthens the idea of ripeness as a necessary pre-cursor for reaping.

The second problem is more of a practical one. Though I firmly believe that the Church should never act towards someone as though they were a lost cause, it is patronising to treat all people as though they were actively seeking God. I can readily think of some people I know who would be extremely affronted by the suggestion that though they didn't recognise it they were needing or seeking God—with the added implication that their lives are somehow deficient. Though I actually believe that life without a faith in God is lacking, it would be a mistake, I think, to treat everyone as though they were actively seeking. We must beware a kind of arrogance in our treatment of those without belief. It is clear that there are many people who at least appear to have found some meaning in life without a faith in God. Though I don't pretend to understand it, there is something in the idea of a 'secular' spirituality.

However, at Willow Creek the basis of their treatment of unbelievers is the statement that 'lost people matter to God'. In consequence, all who do not know Christ are regarded as 'seeker' potential. It's important to understand that because I think within many church cultures outside the USA the term 'seeker' delineates something slightly different. The term 'seeker' in UK church culture is someone who articulates an interest in spiritual things or a desire to find some meaning in life—or even someone who has shown some sort of goodwill towards the Church. It's for this reason I am happier to use the term 'unchurched' for our own culture because I think it is the nearest approximation to the American use of the word 'seeker'. It certainly implies an evangelistic concern for a wider group than simply the 'fringe'.

But are there any things which might be said to describe those 'beyond the fringe' who are more likely to respond to the Gospel? The characteristics of those who might be 'ripe' for the Gospel include:

- a sense of dis-ease with the 'givenness of life' as it is;
- a desire to explain the world as it is experienced;
- a recognition that left only with my own inner resources to deal with life's problems, I am in a very fragile state;

- a feeling of vulnerability often hastened, for instance, by illness or bereavement, conception, birth or relationship difficulties;
- a state of loneliness, physically or emotionally;
- those whose 'life-script' has given them a sense that they are unacceptable;
- those who are looking for a new start or 'clean sheet'.

If any of these characteristics have a hint of truth about them then a couple of things emerge. Firstly, that different approaches will be required. Those people who are seeking to make sense of the way life is, might well require a more 'apologetic' approach. Those who have been damaged by life's experiences will require a more pastoral approach, where the love of God is reflected by church members.

Secondly, it becomes clear that relational or 'friendship' evangelism is a key tool in all cases. Those believers who model the message in their everyday life and particularly in their relationships with unbelievers are likely to be the effective evangelists in tomorrow's Church.

The World of the Unchurched

Inevitably, any attempt to address such a question runs the danger of over-generalisation. However, in a context where many Christians wax lyrical about the Incarnation—the Spirit of God in the world—as a model for mission, it must be said that a lot of missionary strategies appear to show a wholesale unwillingness to grapple with the real world at which they are directed.

In the next Chapter we shall look at ways of gathering some hard data upon which to base our strategies. A basic fact we have to wake up to is that we live in a world where a good many people will openly tell you that you don't have to go to church to be a Christian (nominalism) or that you don't have to be a Christian to know God (pluralism).

What we also need to understand is that most people are not lying around on Sundays with little to do or with restricted options. Here in the UK in the light of recent Parliamentary debate I have little doubt that Sunday shopping will play a larger part in people's lives. Sunday sport is now a big factor. Indeed most junior soccer and junior rugby is run on Sundays. Very often there is live sport on the TV. But you don't just have to like sport to be entertained on a Sunday. Where I live the car-boot sale is very popular. Indeed, people are queuing to get in from about 7 am onwards! The sale caters, rather poorly from what I observe, for literally hundreds of people, all on the look-out for a bargain.

The advent of more women at work has meant that weekends are now prime time for house cleaning and renovation. Presumably that's why the do-it-yourself centres were amongst the first to bend the law on Sunday trading. They realised that there was a market out there waiting to be won. There are Sunday papers to be read, there are lawns to be cut, there are cars to be cleaned, there's family leisure to be enjoyed and the list could go on and on and on...

I mention all this only to highlight that there are a thousand good reasons why Sunday attendance at churches is under real pressure. Even our committed people sometimes find the world's agenda a little too tempting. Without condoning absenteeism amongst the committed I can understand the temptation to give church a miss when there's such a great range of options to choose from.

Quite rightly some will ask what my preoccupation, as a minister, with getting people into church is all about. Such people will tell me that it's far more likely that we will attract people to evangelistic events beyond the church. I will be the first to agree with you, but, recalling that the goal of our evangelism is to see unbelieving people become fully devoted followers of Jesus Christ rather than just 'get converted', I think you can't ignore the issue of church.

> **The problem is that much of our church life is geared to believers with a strong feel for Christian culture, which people without that background will find very difficult to identify with.**

The World of the Church – digging out the 'rubble'

It has long been appreciated by many of those people who have a concern for evangelism that the Church has more often been a hindrance than a help in the business of mission. That said, it is one thing to have some feel for the problem, it is another thing to do something about it. Increasingly I come across Ministers who are feeling frustrated by the recognition that the Church as it is will not help much in the task of winning lost people for Christ. This is matched by church memberships who are largely anxious to maintain what they have. A senior pastor admitted to me recently that he

Who are the Seekers? 47

had been 'uncomfortable' with the Church for years as an aid to mission.

It's easy for us to talk in terms of 'a church for the unchurched' and 'a church without walls' yet continue to model a 'club' mentality. A biblical phrase that's stuck with me over the years comes from the Old Testament Book of Nehemiah. Nehemiah was the man whom God charged with the task of rebuilding the broken walls around the city of Jerusalem. Having started the task the people of Judah had a complaint to make. In Nehemiah 4:10, they say, 'The strength of the labourers is giving out, and there is so much rubble that we cannot rebuild the wall.'

I've always felt that was a prophetic word for the Church. For the task of mission is made even more exhausting by the 'rubble' that exists in our churches. It's what Dan Postierski in his excellent book, *Re-inventing Evangelism*[1] calls the baggage of church life. In a Chapter called 'Embracing God's Diversity' he categorises the components of church life under the headings of, *treasures, baggage and garbage*. (He goes on to attribute the idea for this categorisation to a monk from a monastery in Minnesota!)

What is this rubble that gets in the way? I have an awkwardness about talking about it because for many committed members it's a very important part of their Christian devotion. Oddly, in many churches, members are far less ruffled by the public denial of biblical truth than they are about having these somewhat peripheral aspects of their faith questioned.

Hesitantly I offer the following, merely as some of the 'rubble' that makes the task of mission to a post-Christian society even more exhausting.

48   *Reaching the Unchurched*

- organ music
- chanting
- ancient language
- religious jargon
- elaborate ritual
- hugging each other
- over-enthusiasm
- irrelevant and lengthy preaching and prayers
- robes
- taking collections
- books that are difficult to find your way around
- welcoming teams that 'invade your personal space'
- unannounced and unpredictable changes of posture
- arm-waving.

Of course you can reject this list and find some unbelievers who will love elaborate ritual or choral music or arm waving. I'm not arguing that in every social context everything on this list might have to go. Surely, however, none of these components of rubble are non-negotiable if we are to build churches appropriate for the unchurched. It's certainly true in the building process that some rubble can be used as ballast upon which new structures can be erected. I am very aware that there are certainly those who will only find Christ in more formal worship whilst a 'rave in the nave' will attract others. It seems very likely, however, that most of those who find Christ through formal ritual probably already have some kind of cultural 'handle' on Christianity. The point about rubble is that sometimes we have to remove it in order to get on with the job of rebuilding.

It worries me that while we appear so defensive about the rubble we are maintaining and reinforcing, there is a widely-held view that our Christianity is exclusive and irrelevant. Willow Creek had the advantage in those early days of commencing as a 'rubble-free' community. Many other church leaders will not start with that advantage. They will face the real but necessary challenge of trying to clear some of that rubble in order to begin the real task of mission amongst the many unchurched people around. As anyone with experience will tell you, moving rubble can be an exhausting and demoralising task—but it has to be done. We prefer maintenance to demolition!

The Culture Chasm

What clearly emerges is a great gap between the world of the unchurched and the world of the Church. I'm not too sure how many churches have genuinely tried to look at that gap. Most of our clergy have been trained to operate in a different climate. They are described as 'professionally trained'. They have been taught to 'run churches'. The appropriateness of this in the present climate is under question. Perhaps a new model will emerge? There is talk of the 'pastor-evangelist' and the 'pastor-teacher' around at present which sounds promising.

Of course all this puts immense pressure on church leaders. I know from personal experience that when I landed in a church after training in the mid-1970's it was a shock. In some ways it seemed like a conspiracy! Very quickly I realised that there was an immense amount to learn and quite a lot to re-learn for the task of engaging in mission in a suburban south London church. Whether the situation in colleges has changed very much I don't know. I do know that the need for training church leaders who can relate to this post-Christian context in which we find ourselves is actually very important.

Whether we like it or not, it's fair to say that when it comes to the world of the unchurched we have to show an appreciation for the kind of things that they are doing when we are in church on Sunday. Because Sunday seems to be such prime time for people to do other things, it might be worth seriously investigating whether another day other than Sunday might be more appropriate. This is not to suggest anything either new or heretical. Many churches have a midweek service already – though often at times when the majority of people are at their paid employment. As has been mentioned, the initial research at Willow Creek revealed that within their own culture Sunday mornings would be the best 'slot' for their seeker service. That's precisely why they asked their committed membership to worship in the midweek.

I assume that some churches will be put under another kind of pressure by the new Sunday Trading legislation. A good many town centre churches do not have their own car park. Because of this they have relied on the relative quiet of Sunday to park cars on the local streets or in local car parks. If Sunday trading becomes big – and the signs are that it will – then parking is going to become a headache. It would be easy for churches to get angry about this.

On the other hand, the fact that there are a lot more people around town on a Sunday can be viewed positively. It might provide for those who dare to 'break the mould' and deploy some imagination an interesting opportunity for a bit of outreach. Maybe a 'shopper's service' with free coffee and doughnuts thrown in might catch the shopper! It's that kind of invasion of the secular world which I believe will start to close this culture chasm across which very few unchurched people cross from one direction and even fewer Christians cross from the other side.

Bishop Nigel McCulloch wrote recently, 'We are still a long way from achieving the massive switch to missionary mode that the Lambeth Conference of 1988 asked for…there has been an over-emphasis on the importance of making churches user-friendly. Far more urgent is the need for a genuinely prophetic and evangelistic engagement with the world. As the Gospels clearly indicate, mission is not about keeping churches going, rather, it is about extending the Kingdom.'[2]

The Bishop's point is well made, but while the Church persists in churning out leaders who are taught to 'keep churches going' there will be a continued sense of frustration along the lines that the Bishop describes. For them the **only** starting point will be to try and make their churches a little more user-friendly. I share the Bishop's limited enthusiasm for such a lightweight response. On the other hand it may be part of a process. A process which will open the eyes of those who at present are struggling to engage in mission, and help them see a bigger picture, which will give them a new confidence to engage prophetically and evangelistically with the world.

I do think, notwithstanding the need in our churches to repent of our lack of interest in the unchurched, that the only feasible starting point for a lot of churches will be to review their user-friendliness. For many churches this will be a positive contribution and certainly a good place to begin. The transformation to a mission mode is

52 *Reaching the Unchurched*

a huge leap for churches reared on decades of maintenance mode. We shall all constantly need to remind ourselves that, 'For God nothing is impossible' (Luke 1:37).

Notes

1. *Re-inventing Evangelism*, Donald C. Posterski (IVP [USA]), 1989.
2. Taken from an article headed 'No Substitute' by Rt Rev'd Nigel McCulloch, Bishop of Wakefield in 'Decade Matters' in the Church Times 7/1/94.

4

Starting the Process

The $64,000 question in the deployment of any new strategy is where to start. In most of our churches the process of transformation from the traditional club mind-set to a mission-minded congregation will meet with a wide range of local opinion varying from enthusiastic support to overt hostility. The task of leadership in this process cannot be overstated. The Bible encourages us to 'Buy truth and do not sell it; get wisdom, discipline and understanding' (Proverbs 23:23). Leaders who seek God's wisdom are vital. At the same time we are all encouraged when we lack wisdom to ask God for it with the assurance that He gives it (James 1:5).

In a frontier situation the wisdom to know **where** to begin is crucial. Time and time again in parish ministry I came to see that the only starting point is to begin in prayer with the leadership team. Praying together for clarity of vision; praying for the conviction of the Holy Spirit to give us passion for that vision and asking for the wisdom to articulate the vision with that clarity and passion to the church membership; praying for the protection of the leadership team and the church at a time of strategic significance.

One great danger, of which I have some personal experience, is the temptation to want to see a quick pay-out from some new strategy. It's a bit like what economists call 'short-termism'. It's trying to take a short-cut to success—a desire to see quick results from a new strategy. My experience tells me that this kind of wild rushing into new things is real folly. It results in the kind of churches which we all know. Churches which rush from strategy to strategy without any proper investment in any of them. The result tends to be exhaustion and disillusionment rather than the intended goals of life and growth.

A very important part of the process is what I call 'vision-casting'. Taking time and care to explain a new vision and the strategies that we envisage to release that vision to the church membership. Allowing members time and space to respond so that any proposed strategy is 'owned' by them. The quadrant in figure 1 may help to illustrate this.

The task of leadership is, in part, the task of taking an **unowned** idea and seeing it nurtured so that it becomes an **owned** action. The illustration attempts to demonstrate that if we try and short-cut the process of casting the vision with church members then what will result is unowned action—the exhausted efforts of a few enthusiasts trying to press on regardless. Much better is the kind of vision that is owned by the great majority of the church in such a way that their gifts and resources are enthusiastically employed in the realisation of that vision.

In a way, all this is very basic. Yet, time and time

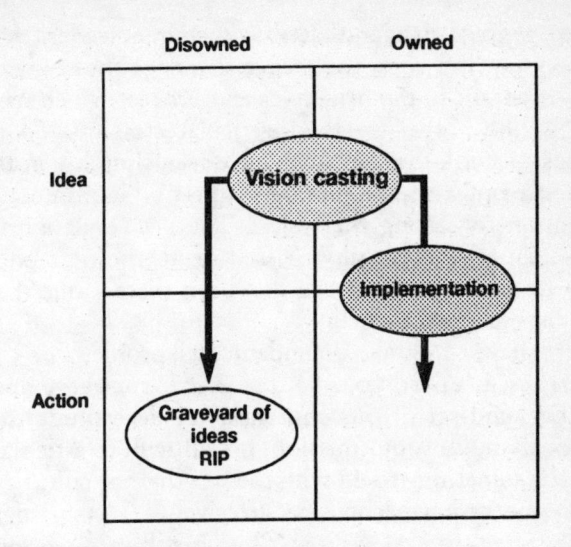

	Disowned	Owned
Idea		Vision casting → Implementation
Action	Graveyard of ideas RIP	↓

again, I see churches which have made this error. That is, the error of trying to implement strategies without proper attention to vision-casting. The reasons for this are no doubt complex, but I think that part of it lies in that worldly hunger, which is present in many of us, for success. Not that a desire for success is entirely or necessarily wrong, but it can so quickly become a worldly obsession. Such church leadership rarely sees the distinction between Kingdom-building and empire-building.

Attacking the Mind-set

What most people associate with the Willow Creek model is the centre-piece strategy of their seeker service. Indeed it is the seeker service that most people take home with them from Willow Creek conferences.

I see a great danger that many church leaders will simply try and copy the seeker service without giving any attention to the principles and process which have led Willow Creek to this particular strategy. To be honest, I think that already I have seen churches in the UK attempt a seeker service without giving time and attention to casting the vision. The net result is that these churches have now passed on to the next good idea to try. It's what I call the 'been there, done that, got the tee-shirt' mentality.

We have, I think, a fundamental problem in our churches. It's partly our heritage and it runs very deep in the mind-set of our churches. It's an attitude that seriously inhibits our mission. It's difficult to articulate but it's something to do with the fact that the culture of this country has become progressively less 'Christian' in this century and yet the Church still seems to act, not least in mission, as though the world was the same as it was fifty years ago. Many of the new breed of churches which have hit the church scene in the last thirty years seem to share this somewhat reactionary outlook.

With such a limited mind-set the net result is that the Church becomes more and more marginalised. The 80-plus per cent of people who know little or nothing of the claims and teaching of Jesus Christ continue to expand as the Church continues to contract. Sadly, the missionary strategies we do deploy are largely 'more of the same'.

> **The terrible thing is that we ignore almost totally the fact, though we would mostly deny it, that we have ceased to be a missionary church.**

Despite the fact that considerable money has been spent on mission and the fact that conferences on mission and evangelism proliferate, there is still plenty of evidence to suggest, at the level of the local church, that most church members are not terribly concerned about sharing their faith with their neighbours.

Until this situation is seriously addressed our missionary efforts will be greatly inhibited. To begin to think about where we start in all this is to ask how we might challenge the prevailing Christian mind-set and help believers to see that they, quite literally, might be the only hope for some of their non-believing friends. For unless this mind-set is rejected for the lie that it is, we shall continue to preach our evangelistic messages to the already convinced.

Concern for the Lost

The starting point is therefore the goal of convincing church members that they have a fundamental part to play in the Church's mission. Teaching will play an important part of this process. A good starting point might be in small groups to discuss a basic question such as, 'What stops us from sharing our Christian experience with our friends?' The fruits of such discussion could provide us with a teaching series on the subject. However, one course of sermons will hardly change the missionary culture of our churches. It may take a long time for Christians in UK churches to, 'bite the bullet'. The Willow Creek seven-step philosophy begins with two principles that form the basis of all that follows. Importantly they highlight the involvement of all church members in mission.

People will need great help with all this. They will need to grasp the theological statement that 'lost people matter to God'. They will need to see that because of God's concern for lost people, the lost will be important to His Church. They will need courage if they are to get involved in this. Just to know that most Christians are scared when it comes to trying to share a verbal witness or offer an invitation to an evangelistic event to their non-Christian friends is re-assuring. The opportunity to talk about these fears together in small groups and to share experiences is a good way of helping people to come to terms with their anxieties.

They will need encouragement to learn to rely on God's resources; to pray regularly for courage and for their non-believing friends is really important. It's something that **all** Christians can do from day 1. To do so requires us to accept two basic principles. Firstly, a belief that God answers the prayers of His people. Secondly, a commitment to our non-believing friends. Most Christians would not quibble with the first; many would appear not to be too concerned about the second.

A God of Love and Justice

It is said that one of the missing components of contemporary mission theology is the fact that people no longer seem to believe in a God who judges (Hebrews 9:27). In our pluralist, relativist culture the idea of a God who might punish sin is regarded as barbarous by many. In a world where tolerance is worshipped as a 'mega-virtue' the idea of a God who might be intolerant of sin is viewed as inconceivable. Indeed there are many Christians, some of whom would describe themselves as evangelicals, who seem to no longer believe in such things. Many of these people are happy, it seems, to leave the eternal destiny of their friends and relatives to the somewhat sentimental and unbiblical hope that God in the final analysis, will turn a blind eye towards unbelief.

The net result is that many modern Christians do not really see the need for evangelism. The overriding idea that God is love (which indeed He is), and that He is slow to answer and abounding in mercy (which indeed He is), seems to have blunted the cutting edge of motivation for mission. If, in the final analysis, all will be well for all people, then the very real question arises, 'What's the point?'

This is not a plea for a return to the 'hell-fire and damnation preaching' so readily and rightly rejected by many Christians today. It is rather a concern to explain that our theology for mission must have as its basis a biblical understanding of God.

True, the Bible reveals a God who is loving and slow to anger. But that same Bible also reveals a God who is concerned for justice. It seems to me that it is this concern for justice that means we cannot easily sidestep the idea of a judgement. To use an example, our commitment to a cure will depend on our understanding of the seriousness of the illness we have. If we feel that our illness is of the kind that will get better without treatment then we will not be overly committed to the cure the doctor offers us. If, however, we understand that our sickness is serious then we would be foolish to discount the cure.

The Need to Repent of Sin

The problem we have in our churches is that there is a reluctance to concede that the human race is chronically sick. An unwillingness to accept that sin is serious. The results are twofold. Firstly, that our commitment to Jesus Christ and His atoning death on the Cross as the only cure for the sickness of humanity is wavering—there is I perceive a greater willingness amongst preachers to speak about things like 'low self-esteem' rather than sin. Secondly, Christians put evangelism a long way down their list of priorities if it appears at all.

The need we have in this matter of altering the mind-set is the need to return to some biblical teaching about the nature of God and the nature of humanity. This is not something which is short term in that it won't happen overnight. It is correcting an imbalance which has probably existed for the greater part of this century.

Let me reiterate what I'm saying here. I'm not suggesting that we return to ranting and raving at unbelievers from our pulpits. That would cut very little ice in the situation we find ourselves in today. I am arguing that unless Christians understand that the biblical prognosis for unbelievers is extremely dubious then their commitment to evangelism will be minimal. Before our membership will get serious about taking responsibility for influencing their non-Christian friends, they will need to be convicted of the need to do so. That much seems obvious.

Finding out the Facts

Because a good many Christians have been absorbed into a Christian culture, they find it hard to recollect what it was like before they became Christians. In many churches the age profile of the congregation, weighted towards the elderly, means that a lot of people who are Christians have been Christians for a very long time. Even if they could remember what it was like to be an unbeliever, their memories would have little to offer in terms of formulating a strategy for mission today because the world has changed a lot since then. The consequence of all this is that when Christians attempt to formulate a strategy for mission they often find themselves planning on the basis of their fantasy about what unchurched people will find appealing rather than on hard data.

Often what we think is attractive to unbelievers has the very opposite impact. Recently I was asked to speak at an 'outreach service' on a housing estate near to where I live. The venue was a local community centre and the church concerned had been doing a monthly outreach service in the building over a period of time. It became rapidly clear to me that those gathered were mostly Christians apart from three teenage girls who wandered in from the street to see what was going on.

The 'outreach' consisted of several choruses heartily sung by the Christian congregation, many of whom raised their hands in worship and spoke half-audibly in tongues between choruses. There was an excellent drama performed by the young people followed by a dance in which members of the congregation were grabbed from their seats to join the dancers in what I can only describe as a 'Christian Conga'. I decided that the message I had prepared was irrelevant and opted for a message more relevant for a Christian congregation. It was difficult to avoid the conclusion that what was being done on this occasion in the name of 'outreach' was simply a group of Christians doing their own thing in a different venue. After the service I spoke with a senior lay-leader about how seriously he felt the attempt at outreach was. He admitted with sadness that he had wondered whether what was being done was appropriate for outsiders, but that those who went enjoyed themselves.

Of course, it's easy to be critical. I have to say that however misguided I felt this church was about what constitutes outreach, there was a commitment amongst the Christians there which was exemplary. At least they were having a go at doing something, which is more than can be said for some churches. However, this experience serves to illustrate that we need to think very carefully about what we are doing when we step out in mission. To be well-intentioned is not enough.

Using a Questionnaire

At Willow Creek a lot of time at the beginning was spent trying to get some hard data. This was used to try and create the kind of church which would be welcoming to unbelievers and which would surprise them by upsetting their prejudices about church. They did this by door-to-door research with questionnaires which attempted to uncover what the non-churchgoing public found so difficult about church. The research provided some important clues.

The kind of popular perceptions that people in their context revealed were that many of the unchurched feared that the Church was after your money. Willow Creek countered this by never asking visitors to give at the offertory. Today at Willow Creek, visitors are actively discouraged from contributing. Some people perceived that the music in churches was old-fashioned and out of date. Willow Creek countered this by providing music excellently performed in a contemporary idiom. Of course the preaching was perceived to be boring and irrelevant. Willow Creek countered this by trying to preach biblically about subjects of relevance to the world of the unbeliever.

The point is that it will benefit us in mission in our local churches if we seek to try and discover what people's popularly held prejudices and mis-perceptions of the Church are. Door to door research with a questionnaire is an excellent way into all this. Quite a number of churches have used questionnaires to great effect within their congregations to discover information about the age profile of their congregations or what kind of worship is preferred. Fewer churches have gone on to the streets to discover what their non-members think about them. The results can be staggering.

In the last church at which I was Minister a door to door survey held in a part of the parish in which church attendance was minimal was quite revealing. When asked the question 'If there were a small group of people meeting together to learn the basics of the Christian faith would you be interested in attending?' a majority of over 50 per cent responded by saying 'Yes'. This piece of research was an invaluable encouragement to a member of staff who had been working with 'Enquirers Groups'. The fruit of his labours is a good number of adult converts to the Christian faith. An example of this kind of questionnaire is in Appendix II at the back of this book.

Many churches will wonder whether they have the expertise to put together a questionnaire which is appropriate. It may well be worth approaching the local College of Further Education. I have discovered that teachers of statistics are usually only too willing to give help and advice on the design of a questionnaire. Often they will 'adopt' such an exercise because the prospect of a live project for their students is preferable to a theoretical one. In some instances they may be willing to give some training to researchers who volunteer from the local church. The whole thing can actually be great fun and helps church members to get on the streets doing something that may provide you with some keys to open your church to unchurched people.

How to be Realistic in your Own Locality

There is a need to remain realistic in all this. It may well be that some of the things you discover as a result of your research are impossible to deliver. The constraints of people's available time and other resources might mean that some good ideas are out of the question. It's important that someone helps you interpret the results of your research. Sometimes it's what people **don't** say that is important. I suppose that the key question in the light of collecting some hard data is something like, 'What's the most important thing we could realistically do as a result of this research?' What is clear is that it's important not to attempt too much at once. The results of your research may be the basis of a five-year strategy—or even longer. Patience is a fruit of the Holy Spirit!

It's important to understand that Willow Creek, today a huge local church, was once a smallish church plant driven by the energy of a few young people who shared a common vision. True, they had the apparent advantage of being an independent church without the apparent baggage of church tradition. Nevertheless their resource base was not huge. To run away from the Willow Creek model on the basis of scale is to forget this. Of course it's not possible overnight to copy the vast range of ministries that Willow Creek is able to offer today. Neither is it likely that a lot of churches will readily be able to reproduce the sophistication that Willow Creek is able to model in their seeker services today. But we can all start somewhere in our own way.

Let me stress again that the starting point is not to begin with trying to copy a North American product. In a way it's a lot more scary than that. It's praying that the Holy Spirit of God will transform the mind-set of local Christians away from a preoccupation with maintenance to a missionary mind-set, through teaching, through prayer, through all the spiritual strategies that God has put at the disposal of His Church. It is from this mission mind-set that a generation of appropriate seeker-targeted churches will arise. This process will take time.

I'm glad that in the UK there has not been a proliferation of seeker-targeted churches. Had this happened I think it would be an example of the danger that this chapter is basically about. That is the danger of simply copying a product without giving attention to the principles and process that need to be properly worked through before we embark on any action.

My hope is that in the UK and in Australia and in South Africa and wherever there is a growing conviction that the Willow Creek model deserves serious examination, there are churches that are busy now seeking to cast the vision. Helping local Christians to see that without their ministry the missionary strategy of the church is flawed. Beginning to ask what kind of local church will be needed to assist Christians in the task of bringing their friends to Christ and seeing them nurtured through to becoming fully devoted followers.

Having the courage, imagination and patience to allow this process to work its way through. Who knows—two or three years from now we might begin to see the advent of churches which are equipped for the task?

Strategy is Important

Even to use terms like 'strategy' is to run the risk of alienating some church communities. To them such words belong to the board rooms of commercial enterprises or to government 'think-tanks' rather than to church committees. However, it is possible to show that when it comes to mission the apostle Paul had a strategy which he regularly implemented.

It's noticeable that when he went to a new city on his missionary journey's he seemed to employ the same strategy regularly. On arrival he would always go first to the synagogue (see Acts 13:14; 14:1; 17:1; 17:10). Presumably, in Paul's thinking it was in the synagogue that the 'warm' contacts would be found. Here were Jews who believed in God and were familiar with the Old Testament Scriptures. Paul's focus on mission in the synagogue was to open the Old Testament Scriptures and seek to prove from the scriptures that Jesus was the awaited Messiah. This tactic mostly had two immediate results. Firstly, that some people were always persuaded; secondly, that there was nearly always hostility displayed towards Paul and his various companions.

Acts 17:16-34 provides us with a fascinating perspective on Paul's preaching to a Gentile audience at the Areopagus in Athens. A group of Stoic and Epicurean philosophers began a dispute with Paul having heard Paul preach in the market place, where he had been speaking about the good news of Jesus and about the resurrection. They then took Paul to a meeting of the Areopagus, a sort of philosophical 'ideas market'.

Here Paul's strategy appears to be quite different. The scriptures are not opened, though scriptural truth is certainly proclaimed. The basis of Paul's argument in this context is that the God who is the Creator is too big to be imprisoned in temples built by human hands. That this God who also created the whole human race created human beings with a spiritual appetite that only He could nourish. That He can be found because, 'He is not far from each one of us.' Paul quotes one of their own poets and ends with warnings about idolatry and about God's impending judgement.

It would be easy to overdo this point, but nevertheless it does seem that Paul worked with a well-developed strategy in mission. He'd thought about where to begin – with 'warm' contacts. He'd thought about the content of his message for such contacts. He was prepared to take the Gospel into the market place and when given an opportunity he seemed to be willing to 'have a go'. It seemed that Paul had also given some thought to the kind of people that he was speaking to. His observations about their religious adherence and culture were taken account of in his message and most significantly, some became believers.

A strategy for mission is important. Careful thought about the way we preach in relation to the audience we have is critical. Having some feel for the local culture is helpful. Stepping out into the world of the unbeliever is scary but rewarding. Having found out the facts it's important that we plot a strategy which takes account of those facts. Time invested in this is crucial. It's much better to work out a strategy which has some basis in reality than rush into the next 'good idea'. Attention to detail at the planning stage is important.

To be realistic, in most churches the starting point will be strategies aimed at moving the church away from a maintenance mind-set to a mission mind-set. A good many of the evangelistic events I have attended have been absolutely excellent. The problem however, has been that the Christians had not invited their unbelieving friends.

Offering the Invitation

This problem is still the biggest to overcome. How can we seek to try and encourage our fellow church members to invite their unbelieving friends? I take it that there are a variety of reasons why many Christians don't do this. The following is a summary of the factors involved which have emerged when I have been talking to groups of Christians.

1. Fear that their friends will be embarrassed by what they experience. This can mean a real fear of emotional manipulation by the speaker or a time of worship which is embarrassingly over-enthusiastic. It's what I've heard somebody call the 'cringe factor'.
2. A fear that friends will be alienated by an invitation that they don't really want and that a refusal will bring an awkwardness into the relationship.
3. Leaving it too near the time of the event to offer the invitation because it took us a long time to get round to bucking up the courage to invite someone. 'When we finally asked they had something else planned.'
4. A worry that we might be thought to be religious fanatics.

Part of this will be resolved by us committing ourselves to guarantee, as far as is humanly possible, that what will take place will be non-embarrassing and enjoyable for those who attend. I'm not suggesting that the message be watered down but that the context in which the message will be delivered should be 'cringe-free'. I even wonder if, to give people confidence in the event, we ought not to do a 'dry-run' of the event so that people could get the message that here is something they could bring their friends to.

For obvious reasons when special venues are being hired at great expense such a dry-run might have to take place in a different venue. It may even be worthwhile having some feedback after a dry-run so that adjustments could be made where serious and constructive criticism is being offered. There would certainly not be the space for the kind of comment that used to make me hopping mad after a good quality evangelistic event, 'if we'd known it was going to be this good we'd have brought our friends.'

Practical Details

It may be helpful for Christians to have an evening's training on the theme of invitation offering. Interestingly, many of my friends who always go out of their way to try and bring their unbelieving friends to evangelistic events, put alongside my own experience, confirms the common conclusion that people who refuse invitations do not suddenly become hostile or angry. No doubt if the invitation was pushed after an initial refusal people would get cross. But then so would I if faced with a similar scenario. Our fear that offering an invitation will result in a relationship breakdown is more likely our own fantasy.

Publicity needs to be out early—perhaps eight weeks before an event, maybe longer—and needs to be attractive and handleable. Frankly, A4 duplicated sheets will not do for the 1990's and most of our membership know it. Something that looks like an invitation will be helpful. It needs to be clear in what it is trying to communicate with dates, times and venues prominent. Make sure the full facts are given. Never attempt to trick someone into attending what appears to be a social event, but is really an evangelistic event. They will find it difficult to trust you again.

If you are to give a title to the talk make sure it's a good one which is interesting and arresting rather than dull and boring. If the purpose is evangelism avoid titles that are in-house such as 'Cross-purpose?' Many people today won't get the clever play on words. Also worth avoiding is jargon titles like, 'Redemption Revisited!'

Again, it's worth giving early and regular encouragement to the membership to make sure they don't leave their invitation too late. I've been thinking recently—given the world in which we live—whether there is some kind of incentive that could be offered to Christians who bring an unbelieving friend to an outreach event. I'm not suggesting a weekend in Paris for two for the person who brings the most people to outreach events over a period (though frankly, it seriously crossed my mind). But I'm sure that there's some mileage in this line of thinking if handled sensitively.

As to the charge that we might be labelled 'religious fanatics' I find it difficult to comment. Except to say that given a choice between running the slim risk of such a label or the likelihood of being a Christian who is not instrumental in the conversion of my unbelieving friends, it's a 'one-horse race'. On some things we just have to bear the cost of our calling!

The Management of Change

It can probably be said with some certainty that our churches will not respond with overwhelming enthusiasm to attempts to transition them from maintenance to mission-minded communities. Interestingly, because the club mentality exists in so many of our churches, members will resist such attempts. In many ways it's understandable. To extend the club analogy, it's a little bit like asking people who joined a chess club to jettison chess in favour of soccer in order to gain numbers. With some justification the members of the chess club will point out that they didn't join up to play soccer. Their basic desire and need to play chess will be undermined in the attempted transition.

All this means that transition of any kind means careful management. This requires leadership which understands the management of change. Indeed, I would recommend that leadership teams in churches should together attend one of several courses available on this vital aspect of management. Such an investment could save a lot of unnecessary hassle created by mismanagement.

When most leaders return from the latest conference with a new vision and idea, reactions vary. Some sit and listen and adopt the view, 'Smile and he or she will get over it.' Others are more readily vocal in their opposition – 'We came here to play chess.' Yet others have a more 'let's wait and see what happens' attitude. Very few readily climb aboard with enthusiasm.

To Change or Start Afresh?

It's on this point that some of the teaching at Willow Creek needs careful scrutiny because its basis is in a different historical setting. The basic message that Willow Creek sends out on this matter of transition is, 'If you're seeking to transition an existing church into a seeker-driven church – DON'T DO IT!' The American advice is to start afresh with a new church. The reason offered for this is primarily a catalogue of disaster stories involving American churches where the pastor attempted to transition, usually far too quickly, an established church into a seeker-driven church.

In the earliest days of Willow Creek those of us who took some responsibility for sharing the vision of seeker-driven churches followed the line of caution in this matter of transition. More recently and looking at the churches which are beginning to move towards a more seeker-targeted outlook a very different picture seems to be emerging here in the UK. That is to say, the early caution on this matter of transition seems to be less relevant in the UK than in the USA.

Though these are still early days, if this is true, it means that there is an even greater need to prepare church leaders here for the process of managing change. The reasons for this difference are not easy to explain. It may simply be true that some of the disasters spoken of in the USA were attempts at trying to transition a church without sufficient time spent in explaining and casting the vision. In other words the reason for the failure was to do with bad stewardship of the vision.

The other factor which does make a large difference between the Church in the USA and the Church in the UK is the matter of history. The church over here has been in existence for centuries. To some extent it has learnt to survive by adaptation. To make an obvious point the Church in Europe underwent a reformation which of course is not true of the American Church. I'm not totally convinced by all this, but it might be said that because of our long history we are more able to 'bolt-on' new ideas without having to start afresh. The vast number of independent churches in the USA suggests that there is a much stronger tendency there to starting a new church than adapting to change.

The small amount of evidence is, that if the seeker church movement is to work in the UK it will mostly happen from existing churches. Up to 1992 I knew of only one seeker-targeted church in the UK which was independent of an existing church. All the others were the products of already existing churches. In 1993, however, Michael Fanstone was reporting:

> Across Britain at present there seems to be a move of the Holy Spirit which is encouraging some existing churches to produce offspring. With the blessing of the mother church, they begin some new work in the community for God. At this point, such a group has the freedom to break free from some of the traditions of the parent. With comparative ease, it can make Spirit-led decisions that can help it relate in a meaningful way with the local community. [In some cases this also makes it] a potentially attractive venue for former, previously disillusioned, churchgoers.[1]

The message from Willow Creek in this matter of

transition will therefore need a little more scrutiny outside the USA. This will also be relevant to the churches in Australia and New Zealand as together we seek to unpack this vision in our own contexts.

Hang on in there!

The thrust of this chapter is to try and discourage churches from rushing into this thing without much prayer, careful planning and wise leadership. As they say, 'Rome wasn't built in a day' and neither will seeker-targeted churches emerge overnight. The basic task of moving our churches from maintenance to mission is a slow process which will require both patience and persistence—two important New Testament words. For those churches which pray and plan and those churches which have patience and persistence, the 'plentiful harvest' of which Jesus spoke will become a reality. I for one, can't wait to see it. That is why I seek to deliver this message of encouragement.

Note

1. Michael Fanstone, *The Sheep That Got Away*, Monarch Publications (1993) reproduced in *The Christian Herald*, 11/9/93.

5

The Congregation in 'Mission Mode'

Thus far the point has been stressed that until our congregations realise that they have a part to play in the Church's mission, then we shall struggle to engage with the world in which we find ourselves. It has been deliberately emphasised that the principle task is a basic review of the core values that exist in our local churches. The issue is therefore the complicated task of seeking to adjust the mind-set of our churches in order that the basic culture of the Church will be transformed from a maintenance mode to a mission mode. This is no easy task, but it is nevertheless both a necessary and exciting one. It is vital that church leaders understand this task and manage the vision with both single-mindedness and sensitivity.

What is the Church for?

The simple answer to that question is that the Church is for lots of things.

Reaching the Unchurched

> **The Church is like a bridge between God and man as the varied and practical expression of the body of Christ on earth.**

Different Christians however will interpret this question in different ways and many of their answers would have some foundation in truth. At Willow Creek, as mentioned, their answer to this basic question is their four-fold mission statement. As a church they exist for:

exaltation of the living God;
the **edification** of church members;
the task of **evangelism** in the world;
and **social action**.

It's no bad thing to have a mission statement providing you take some notice of it. The idea of a mission statement is to articulate the core purpose that you hold so that you have a yardstick against which to measure subsequent action.

Working Out the Mission Statement

In the last local church in which I ministered we talked about the 4 W's. The 4 W's stressed our primary objectives for the church which we believed were thoroughly biblical. Basically, they are a variation on the same theme. What is more we preached about them regularly to each congregation in the church so that all our membership would have a basic grasp of these things. If someone asked us about the church then our members would blurt out the 4 W's. They were the guiding, biblical principles upon which our fellowship as believers was based and were as follows:

The Congregation in 'Mission Mode'

- Worship of the Living God.
- Submission to the authority of the Word of God.
- Witnessing in daily life by word and deed to the Son of God.
- The Welfare of people.

Of course each of these statements has to be unpacked and the need to be undergirded with prayer and drenched in the Spirit's power were seen as vital to the fulfilment of any of these purposes. The point being that these objectives are all interconnected. They all require attention. At certain times any one of these objectives might need an extra emphasis but they are all important.

Of course individual Christians will have a particular pull towards any one of them. As a convert to the Christian faith, the statement about witness has always held a particular emphasis in my own Christian walk. Others have their 'switches flicked' by worship or social action. Whatever our individual preferences, it's the task of leadership to keep the church's membership mindful of all aspects of the mission statement. A problem occurs in churches either where the Minister pulls the members in the direction that he has a passion for, and a giftedness in, without giving proper attention to the whole mission statement. Alternatively, problems also occur where for convenience the church lets one or more of its core principles slip off the agenda all together.

How will a church seeking to gear itself into mission mode review these priorities? What kind of qualities will the church in mission mode seek to model? These are very important questions.

To look at Willow Creek solely in terms of its seeker services is to miss an awful lot more about a church which is in mission mode.

To some extent the seeker service is the tip of the iceberg at Willow Creek. Because of its unique style and approach it is the high profile bit that people see. There's a lot more going on in this church in terms of other ministries that are the outworking of their mission statement and their convictions as a church. But it's a church which asks some of the awkward questions of its many sub-ministries in relation to whether they are serving the stated goals of the church.

This seems to me to be in stark contrast to a lot of churches which seem to have the view that all activities must be kept going without question whatever the cost. The idea that many church activities might be reviewed in terms of their effectiveness in serving the church's goals is risky thinking for many. I well remember in a previous church, a former Minister was remembered not for the many innovative and good things he had done, but as the, Minister who 'closed the Mother's Union'. In many churches the 'professional clergy' are hired to keep things running smoothly not to ask awkward questions about whether or not a particular ministry is viable or relevant.

It seems then that in order to 'gear-up' for mission some searching questions will need to be asked of our churches. It's not just a matter of working out some good outreach strategies and trying to implement them. A great deal of what we do will need to be looked at. Some ministries will emphatically continue, others will need to be dropped. The difficulty being, that to continue to maintain ministries which no longer serve the church's goals, is to use wastefully, what in most churches is a limited resource base.

Such questions will test the calibre of those in leadership in our church's sub-ministries—whether their commitment is to the church or to 'doing their own thing'. A senior and wise Christian leader said to me once, 'You can tell a person's real spirituality on the basis of their response, not when you ask them to do something, but rather, on the basis of how they respond when you ask them to stop doing something.'

Building the Body of Christ

The move to events or services for seekers does not diminish the need for worship in which believers can express their love for God in a way which holds meaning for them. The church in missionary mode will work even harder at its worship services for believers—seeking to lift church members into the presence of the Living God. However such churches need to ensure that they have a fuller biblical grasp on what worship is all about. I suspect that many churches reflect an imbalance in this respect.

For most Christians the idea that worship is the 'hallowed hour' on Sundays predominates. The idea that worship is the offering of the whole of our lives is not a common theme with many Christians. For them worship is a weekly escape from the harsh realities of the world outside. It is little wonder that so few Christians are able to make the connection between what they do on Sundays and what they do on the other six weekdays. For quite literally they are worlds apart.

This doesn't mean that the 'hallowed hour' is unimportant; it does mean, however, that in worshipping

God together as His people we are meant to be building up the Body of Christ for servant ministry for the intervening six days. A good many liturgies for Holy Communion end up with what is called a 'dismissal'. A common dismissal contains the words, 'Go in peace to love and serve the Lord.' In other words, 'Go away and get on with it!' The church in missionary mode will leave the church in joyful anticipation, ready for a week of service in Christ's name.

It is in the context of worship that believers will be fed on the exposition of Scripture and by sharing in Holy Communion around the Lord's Table. They will ascribe praise to God in psalms and hymns and spiritual songs. They will pray together for the Church and for the world, for the sick and for anything else they feel constrained to pray for. They may share their experiences as Christians serving in the world. They will exhibit their delight in the presence of God and they know that when they go out of church they go with the sure knowledge that their God goes with them into their homes, businesses, schools, colleges, factories, hospitals, etc.

When a church's theology of worship is reduced to just the 'hallowed' hour on Sundays it invariably, for many, becomes like a 'fix'. A narcotic to help escape from the realities of the world. Very easily such congregations adopt a somewhat negative attitude to the world beyond their Sunday worship. The church as a missionary force is seriously, if not fatally damaged. Whatever we think of the world, and it's certainly easy to be negative, we must not forget that important statement of Christ's that, 'God so **loved the world** that He gave His only Son, (John 3:16).

A Praying Church

The church in missionary mode will be a church which believes that God answers prayers. It may be prayers in church, or prayers in small groups, or prayers said alone. A great danger for missionary churches is that they become technique-based in their attempts to engage with unbelieving people. It's easy to forget that at every point in the life of the Church we rely wholly on the Grace of God as revealed in Jesus Christ. As Jesus Christ said, 'Apart from me you can do nothing'.

In part this will manifest itself in prayers for unbelievers. The results can be awesome. Praying to be led to those who are genuinely seeking can issue in new, often unimagined contacts; sometimes it will result in renewed contacts; sometimes we shall simply start to see our long-standing friends in a new light. There's a health warning here. Don't pray for opportunities unless you're ready to take advantage of those opportunities. If you pray for them—they will happen!

I believe that true prayer begins deep inside us. Somewhere we have to acknowledge our dependence upon God. We begin to pray when we realise that fact. Some of us will have a special gift of intercession. I well remember meeting a woman at the Birmingham 1992 conference who was over from the USA. She told me that intercession was her special gift. She co-ordinated prayer teams to pray continuously throughout the main sessions of the conference and offered teams who would pray with conference delegates who had a particular need. Many of those who were present at that conference would feel that those prayers were wonderfully answered. I hope she goes to lots of conferences.

The importance of praying for our unbelieving friends cannot be overstressed. I have seen people who

I would never have dreamt would become Christians through the faithful, often patient, prayers of others. In some churches 'triplets' are organised where three people meet together regularly to pray for their unbelieving friends. Each member of the group brings three names to pray for and the group spends time together regularly praying for these people. This is just one way that some churches have discovered gets people praying for their non-Christian friends. It's not the only way and I'm sure with imagination we could dream up lots of different ways. The important message is that prayer is vital in a church seeking to be in mission mode.

Unwrapping the Gifts

The New Testament seems very clear that all who are members of the Body of Christ have a gift to be offered in the service of Christ and His Church (1 Corinthians 12). The church which is in the missionary mode will not be a church full of spectators who watch the faithful few exhaust themselves doing ministry. There will be participation at every level by church members.

Willow Creek have a whole ministry department which is in place to help people discover their spiritual gifts and offer them in the service of Christ. Within Willow Creek this ministry is called 'Network Ministry'. To quote from the Willow Creek handbook:

> Network's vision is threefold...to have each believer worship God with service for who He is through who He made them to be...to have every Christian making their unique contribution by serving in a meaningful place of service, being both fruitful

and fulfilled...and to have individual members of the body of Christ honour and serve one another and the world through the local church.

Already across the USA and beyond, churches are finding that Willow Creek's emphasis in this area is dynamically changing their potential in ministry. Willow Creek's Networking materials, with appropriate adaptation, are proving to be a helpful tool in the matter of helping Christians to identify their gifts and use them to serve Christ in the local church. There has been quite a response to their Network materials outside America and right now many churches are seeking to implement programmes that will enable a higher participation level amongst their membership. It's very exciting to meet Christians whose faith has been boosted by the discovery of their ministry gift and the opportunity to exercise it to the glory of God and in the service of His Church.

Bill Hybels is correct when he argues that one of the reasons for the high degree of frustration that many church members experience is the direct result of them not exercising their God-given ministries. There's little doubt that we find a new fulfilment in our Christian lives when we discover and utilise our gifts.

Often churches get hold of this message and undertake a church survey which involves asking members what they think their gifts are or even asking them to fill in a 'grid' which will help them discover what their gift is. This can be helpful, but it can also be dangerous. If you do this kind of thing then you'd better find some 'slots' in which to fit these people's gifts. To identify people's gifts (and sometimes train them in the use of those gifts) and then to leave those gifts unused is very demoralising for those concerned. I firmly believe that the most important thing is to have a common, communicable vision with relevant goals and strategies to which church members can contribute their gifts.

For many people any talk of spiritual gifts is worrying. They have visions of a tongue-speaking, prophesying, swooning chaos! For those people the whole subject of spiritual gifts carries a label marked 'weird'. Well of course it must be said that speaking in tongues and prophesy are listed as spiritual gifts by St Paul (1 Corinthians 12:8-11). It must also be said that some Christians seem to act as though being 'spiritual' and being 'weird' are synonymous. It would seem a shame if the whole area of gifts was marginalised in some churches because of the excesses of a minority in other churches. There are many different kinds of gifts and all will be of value in the life of the church. Most gifts flourish best when exercised as part of a team rather than in isolation.

Some gifts will spiritually develop as we learn to use and extend a particular natural gift we may have in the service of God. People who are naturally gifted musicians often find a new fulfilment in their gift when it becomes something they offer to God in service. The same might be said of many of the more practical gifts that can be offered such as administration or hospitality, even the gift of preaching. These kinds of gifts, in some ways, are easier to handle because they are relatively easy to identify. There are then other kinds of gifts that are a little more difficult because they are less easy to recognise. These gifts will have a more pastoral feel to them. They will be gifts such as discernment or the gift of knowledge or counselling or healing gifts.

It is very clear that a church wishing to function in missionary mode will try to avoid people exercising ministries that they are not gifted to undertake. It may seem a very obvious point, but it's surprising how many people in churches are regularly exercising ministries that they are not gifted for. It's easy to understand why this is. Often in our churches we take the, 'someone's got to do it' option. It may well be that such an option is in urgent need of rethinking.

At Willow Creek they firmly believe that God wants our best. They talk about achieving standards of excellence for God. Whilst it's undoubtedly true that alongside that kind of thinking we need to remember that God still loves us even when we do make a complete 'hash' of things, it's also true that it's better to set our standards high rather than low. Our performance in this sense will be dramatically impeded if we continue to use people in ministries that they are not gifted for.

As a postscript, let me make the obvious point that it's easy to be deluded about where our gifting lies. Whatever I feel my gift is, it is important that others in church leadership affirm that gift. It is also worth pointing out the fact that although a person may be gifted in a particular area, that does not negate the need for training and support in the ministry that ensues from that gifting.

I sense that a lot of churches would benefit from looking at the whole area of the 'giftedness' of their membership again. It was not long ago that I stood in a church where I listened (from close quarters!) to an apparently long-serving member of the choir sing flat throughout the service.

The 'Greenhouse Effect': cultivating growth

Years ago I worked on a Christian Community. My principle task was, with supervision, to look after a huge greenhouse filled with tomatoes. I quickly learnt that the great advantage of a greenhouse is that it creates the kind of conditions in which growth can take place. Indeed, some plants need to be nurtured in the greenhouse in order that when taken to the world outside they can thrive.

It occurred to me that this is what our churches should be like. If the goal of our mission is to make fully devoted disciples of Christ, then part of the task of the church in mission mode will be to create the 'greenhouse conditions' in which new Christians can grow in their faith. At Willow Creek a plethora of different ministries serve the basic goal of creating an environment in which believers can grow in their faith and commitment. These ministries are very varied. On the one hand small Group Bible Studies, which all those who attend Willow Creek are encouraged to join, on the other hand Financial Fitness Seminars where Christians are taught good habits with regard to the use of money. There is a recognition that discipleship is a process rather than a programme and that Christians will need help in order to continue to grow in maturity.

A key area of discipleship training in the church in mission mode is the whole area of teaching Christians early on in the discipleship process about personal testimony and evangelism. I have no research to bear me out, but I would guess that the evangelistic potential of new Christians, who are still in touch with their

The Congregation in 'Mission Mode'   87

previous unchurched culture is considerable. The sooner new Christians can be equipped to get amongst their non-believing friends, the better.

At Willow Creek the Evangelism Ministry Department is a key ministry. Of particular relevance are the Impact Evangelism Seminars which are run on a monthly basis. The purpose of these seminars is:

to motivate believers to build friendships with non-believers;
to instruct them on how to relate what Christ has done in their lives in a natural way;
to present the Gospel message clearly and succinctly;
to prepare them for some of the questions and objections that seekers often raise.

There are four sessions in each course. The titles of the sessions are:

- *Being Yourself*
- *Telling Your Story*
- *Making the Message Clear*
- *Coping with Questions.*

This course is designed for all believers to participate in. For those who feel that they have a particular gift and passion for evangelism there is a Frontline Team. Many who serve the church in other ministries make up this team. The members of this team meet every two months to 'inspire, motivate and challenge each other to greater fruitfulness'.

It is recognised that many people will have their path to spiritual growth blocked by emotional or psychological problems. There is a pastoral counselling centre at the church to enable them to get help and remove the blockage so that they can grow and reach their God-given potential.

The basic point to make here is that the church in mission mode will take the task of discipleship very seriously. Some churches around the world do this already—many do not. This greenhouse effect will be a vital goal in the church in mission mode. There will be a constant teaching emphasis on our need to grow in the faith and very likely we shall have to come to terms with the truth that a diet comprising of the Sunday service alone will not serve the goal of helping people to grow.

Many churches use housegroups as 'mini-greenhouses'. There is much to be said in favour of this. Housegroups can be a very fine strategy in the matter of Christian growth. Many Christians have got an awful lot out of attendance at such groups. The need for co-ordinated and careful planning together with proper support for leaders will enhance their value. Needless to say, housegroups like many other strategies can positively inhibit growth. But I think all churches should seriously consider housegroups as an aid to growth before they reject the idea out of hand. Certainly, individual Christians should make them a very high priority.

Living Together with our Faults and Imperfections

There is little doubt that what a lot of people took away from the Willow Creek Church Leaders' Conference at Birmingham in June 1992, was the Seeker Service concept. But I suspect that there was something else less tangible and harder to describe that people experienced. It was a sense that in Bill Hybels and the team from Willow Creek, there was a Christianity that was visibly evident. The words that people have used to describe it have been words such as 'real' and 'authentic'. There is little doubt that starting with the Senior Pastor and spreading throughout Willow Creek's membership, the importance of Christians modelling a lifestyle which is in line with their beliefs is a priority issue within the church.

Here I suspect they are merely reflecting an undeniably challenging strand of New Testament theology relating to the Church. The way we behave in our relationships, the way we conduct ourselves outside the boundaries of the local church, the way we bring up our children or handle our singleness, the way we care for those who are in need, will all be factors which will assist or inhibit our witness to the Good News about Jesus Christ. There's an awful lot in the New Testament about Christian behaviour. At a time when there seems to be much moral confusion in many so-called 'developed' western societies, the issue of Christian lifestyle becomes central. Sadly, there seems to be as much moral confusion in the Church at times.

If it's true, as Michael Green asserts in his book *Evangelism Through the Local Church* that pragmatism is a characteristic of the framework of the way modern Western society thinks, then this point about lifestyle is a very important area for the Church. He writes:

> This is essentially the age of the pragmatist. Our society abounds in self-help schemes, self-fulfilment programmes, positivism. And many who have dismissed truth as relative are all too willing to ask of any new

idea (yes, especially a new idea), 'Is it any good? Does it work?' Judged by this standard, how does Christianity fare? There is no doubt how the churches at large fare. People who used to attend have voted in massive numbers with their feet. They have not been persuaded that church-going makes any difference. For them it has not 'worked'. That is why they are so quick to call church-goers 'hypocrites'. There is a deep suspicion that these same church-goers are acting a part that is not real. It does not change anything in the ordinary life of work and home. There may be God on Sunday, but not God on Monday.[1]

Here is an important truth for contemporary Christians. It may well be that a lot of the people we are trying to reach are initially, less interested in questions like, 'Is it true?' and more interested in questions to do with whether or not Christianity works. This does not mean that issues of truth become unimportant or that Christian apologetics is a waste of time. It does mean however that if we concentrate solely on these things and ignore the issue of the way we live as Christians we shall rarely engage with the pragmatist culture in which we find ourselves. In a sense we need to discover that an important aspect of apologetics will be the way we behave as Christians.

Here I suspect, the 'power evangelism school' have contributed something important. For if signs and wonders are in evidence in the Christian community then there is some visible evidence to suggest that Christianity 'works'. Much has been written on the subject of power evangelism, a good deal of it highly contentious, but it must be said that this approach has something of an appeal in a pragmatic age.

That said, there must always be a question about solutions which seem to imply that the exercise of the gifts of the Holy Spirit is the authenticating mark of our Christianity. Personally, I am more happy with a theology that leans towards the **fruit** of the Spirit as the authenticating mark of our faith. This means that we should be giving time to develop in our lives, and in consequence in the life of the Church, those qualities of which the apostle Paul speaks in Galatians chapter 5. Qualities which will make a real visible difference in our lives within and beyond the Church.

Mission is certainly a real problem in churches where the moral behaviour of Christians is poor or where relationships are bad. How much more the Gospel is commended when Christians are modelling a lifestyle which has authenticity about it. Authenticity does not mean that we have to be perfect. It means that we don't try to pretend that we are perfect and that we are prepared to own our shortcomings. Certainly it does demand that we avoid a false piety or a sickening self-righteousness, sadly so often equated with Christianity.

You can learn a lot from caricatures. You have only to look at the television to see the way the world perceives Christians. Clergy are viewed as wet and well-meaning, often with a special 'church-speak' tone of voice. Church members are portrayed at best as well-intentioned and naive; at worst they are seen as self-righteous busybodies and bigots, insensitively moral-crusading against anyone and everyone. The hard question for us to face is where does that caricature come from? Did it come only from the creative imaginations of script writers or was the seed of those caricatures sown in the reality of what those scriptwriters had observed? It would be nice if we could vociferously deny that such Christians didn't exist.

Interestingly thumbing through three large books all on the subject of 'evangelism', I couldn't find a single reference to this aspect of the congregation's contribution. On reflection that does seem odd, not least in a world where pragmatism is high on the agenda. Many of us know the truth. When people know we claim a Christian faith, they begin to look a little more closely at us. What will it take for him/her to lose their temper? Is he/she fiddling their tax return like everyone else? How does he/she handle sexual temptation? The list could go on, but the point is clear. Unless we seek to live in a way that honours God by attempting to find a greater consistency between what we claim to believe and the way we behave, the cause of mission is seriously set-back. The church in mission mode will certainly take this challenge with the utmost seriousness.

Willow Creek in their *Purpose and Structure* document actually have a written process for dealing with confrontation. This speaks of their commitment to being a church where relationships count.

> **Too often, in my experience, the ministry of churches is adversely affected by the terrible relationships that exist between church members.**

Those of us who teach the faith should be careful

The Congregation in 'Mission Mode' 93

and constant in our emphasis that where there is disunity and dispute, the Body of Christ is damaged.

Community Care

It's amazing how Christians have found themselves fighting with each other over the issue of social action. The traditional polarisation has formed around, on the one hand, those who see the Gospel as primarily social and, on the other hand, those who see it purely as something to be proclaimed. The argument seems to imply an either/or scenario. Fortunately, I sense in latter years there has been a real change in all this. Those who previously held polarised positions on this subject seem to realise that their original position lacked integrity and good biblical common-sense.

It seems fairly clear that if the church simply becomes a branch of the local social services, then the community at large will happily receive the care offered, but will not likely become Christian disciples without someone 'offering them Christ', as John Wesley put it. It is equally evident that churches which are single-minded in their desire to preach the Gospel without concern for the social environment of the targeted hearers will be viewed as lacking in love.

One of the stated purposes of Willow Creek is 'social action'. The Willow Creek *Leaders' Handbook* expresses the theology of their care in these terms:

> In addition to the proclamation of the gospel, the Church has been commissioned by Christ to extend in the world His own ministry of compassion and of prophetic protest against evil. The Church can never settle for

its own comfort in a world wracked by problems such as moral decay, political corruption and oppression, violence and crime, unjust resource use and wealth distribution, and other social scourges that require solutions and interventions informed by Scriptural imperatives.[2]

At Willow Creek this works out in a variety of different sub-ministries. The following is a list of some of the ministries that run at Willow Creek with a brief description of what they are about.

Community Care Teams: teams of people whose task is to care for the sick and suffering at home or in the hospital.
Exodus Ministry: a specific ministry to support prisoners and their families. There are also programmes to assist ex-offenders re-enter society.
Bereavement Ministry: comfort and help for those experiencing trauma, delayed shock, confusion or difficulties.
Hearing-impaired Ministry: a team of people who can 'sign' for those with hearing difficulties at all Willow Creek's services.
Heritage: members of this ministry commit themselves to sharing the love of Christ with the elderly.
Floral Ministry: members of this team create floral arrangements for the Community Care teams and the Heritage ministry.
Pathfinders: this is a support group for those suffering chronic illness. The ministry offers spiritual and emotional support to the sick, their families and those who give care in such contexts.

The Congregation in 'Mission Mode' 95

A *Social Services* department at Willow Creek also offers a further variety of different ministries. These include food pantries, support for those without paid employment, self-help groups and a *Benevolence Board* which provides financial aid to those who have special needs.

The point is obvious. If the Church is to reflect the ministry of Christ then it will be concerned for those who are in need. It will be a concern for people not primarily because they are prospective church members, but because in God's sight they are of great value. Notwithstanding, it is likely that our attempts at evangelism will be largely futile, if we, the people of God omit to reflect His love into the needy world in which we find ourselves.

The facts are pretty evident in what is called somewhat strangely 'the developed world'. The number of people emotionally damaged through family breakdown; the legacy of the so-called 'permissiveness' of the 1960's; those who feel that they have failed to meet the demands of our 'success-orientated cultures', combine together to create a tidal wave of different needs. Part of our effectiveness in engaging with our culture will be related to our willingness to show the world that we care, not just with passionate rhetoric, but with down to earth practical action. On occasions, despite adverse pressure from within the Church, we shall have to be fearless in speaking out against institutionalised evil.

Postscript

The purpose of this Chapter has been to suggest that to be a Church in mission mode will mean for many of us real change. To enter this 'mode' has wider implications than just adding a few user-friendly evangelistic events. It begins with a change of heart. Alongside this I have sought to demonstrate that there is far more to Willow Creek than simply the Seeker Services. Indeed there is much to be learnt from the way in which this church has, in almost every area of its life, attempted to enhance its mission. Before looking at the Willow Creek Seeker Service that point needed to be made.

Notes

1. *Evangelism through the Local Church* by Canon Michael Green, Hodder and Stoughton, 1990, p. 128.
2. *Willow Creek Church Leaders' Handbook*, p. 10.

6

The Seeker Service

I write a chapter on this subject, somewhat diffidently, because my worry is that people will rush into this without adequate preparation, and without reference to the issue of the mind-set of many Christians considered in the earlier chapters. However, it is important that we take a look at it in terms of what it is we're trying to do and how we achieve the purpose. I'll use the term 'Seeker Service' because that's the term that is espoused at Willow Creek, rather than because I think it's necessarily the best title beyond the USA for reaching the unchurched.

It might be worth reiterating an important distinction at this point. That is the difference between 'seeker-friendly' or 'seeker-sensitive' churches and 'seeker-targeted' churches. The latter are a very rare breed in and outside the USA at present. A seeker-friendly/seeker-sensitive church is one which is attempting, in the context of its established worship menu, to be as open and welcoming to the unchurched as possible. Such churches will have put quite a lot of thought into what they do and why they do it. They are still, however trying to meet the needs of believers and unbelievers in one act of worship.

Seeker-targeted churches by contrast are especially aimed at reaching the unchurched and maturing them into fully devoted followers of Christ. Much of the material in this chapter will hopefully be of interest to both churches seeking to be more seeker-friendly as well as those contemplating seeker-targeted events. For example, quite a number of seeker-friendly churches are attempting some events which are seeker-targeted. The Seeker Service is therefore fundamentally a seeker-targeted strategy.

Presentation rather than participation

The Seeker Service is fundamentally trying to achieve one goal. That is, to provide 'a safe environment for a dangerous message'. The adjective 'safe' here relates to several factors:

- it must engage with the local culture
- it must be 'cringe-free'
- it must give proper attention to detail such as welcoming, handouts, etc.
- it must be free from manipulation, giving space to people to make up their own mind about Christianity.
- it needs to give a priority to biblical and relevant preaching
- it needs to be the right length
- the right kind of venue

One of the big differences is that the emphasis in

seeker-targeted events will be on presentation rather than participation. That will be a problem for many churches, not least those which have grown with a charismatic worship style. One of the great successes of the church in the past twenty-five years has been the charismatic churches. Their basic view was that if you make the centre 'glow' the 'moths' from round about will be attracted by the light. Indeed I can recall that great Christian leader and minister, David Watson using that exact analogy to describe the evangelistic potential of the church. In other words, if you make the worship attractive and participatory, then people will come in.

Of course there was some genuine Kingdom growth in those churches which modelled vibrant worship with this great emphasis upon participation. The emphasis upon participation was welcome, in contrast to the minister-dominated worship characteristic of many churches. However, there is little doubt that much of the growth in these churches was transfer growth—an influx of Christians from other churches who were disillusioned by traditional worship and wanted something fresh and exciting.

One of the real tests I think of the churches reared on 'charismatic worship' will be whether they are prepared to supplement their vibrant worship for something more seeker-friendly. Though in many ways these churches have been created with a dynamic for change built within, they have also been created around a very strong culture of 'needs-based worship'. The limited experience in the UK at present of these churches trying to become more seeker orientated leads to: 'You can change what you like, but don't touch the worship'. It's entirely understandable that people who joined a church as a reaction to traditional forms of worship, will not easily revert to more presentational styles. Yet many unchurched people do find charismatic worship very threatening.

The result is something of an enigma. For the charismatic churches, many of whom are in the forefront of the 'church-planting' movement, may find the shift to genuine seeker-targeted events a major problem. The resultant effect being, that when they plant, they merely reproduce a replica church, which may prove limited in reaching the genuinely unchurched majority.

Let me state quite categorically that worship (for believers), as opposed to Seeker Services (for unbelievers) should certainly be highly participational. But the concept of presentation which I am advocating for non-believers rather than participation, is nothing new. Several years ago John Chapman, formerly Director of Evangelism in the Diocese of Sydney, was arguing that to organise evangelistic events at which unbelievers were asked to sing hymns, the sentiments of which they neither understood nor believed in, was at the very least questionable. It is surely a legitimate issue. On reflection, it seems odd that many high profile crusades have in the past leaned heavily towards hymn singing. Maybe, in what was previously a 'Christian culture' such participation was acceptable. Today's situation is different.

For many, the invitation to 'come and see' rather than 'come and join in' is a far less threatening scenario. Our memberships are more likely to be comfortable with making invitations to their friends to events that are presentation-based. 'Finding out the facts' is both a characteristic and preoccupation of a modern technical culture. Facts about the private lives of politicians are quickly beamed throughout the world. Facts that, in theory, allow you to make the 'best-buy' with your money are a necessary precursor for the modern purchaser. It is reasonable therefore to ask people to 'find out the facts' about Christianity before they reject it out of hand. To offer events where that could happen is entirely appropriate.

A Typical Willow Creek Seeker Service

The items, preaching, songs and drama in a typical seeker service are geared to gain attention in order to provide Christ-centred answers to life or are aimed at sharpening a spiritual hunger for the things of God:

Music–instrumental
Music–vocalist
Congregational song (contemporary)
'Say hello to someone'
Talk–point of common interest
    –e.g. 'Is God really interested in us?'
Drama (comedy)–e.g. interviewing someone with a hang-up about God
Solo (actors still on stage)–e.g. 'Show me the way'
Prayer–for those who search for the truth
    –for those who have found the truth
Notices–next week's message
    –monthly communion (midweek): invite to ALL
    –midweek teaching
    –baptismal classes
    –offerings for the work: 'no need to give'
Offering–music (instrumental)
    –music (soloist)
Message–prayer

- personal everyday experiences/stories
- visual aids: slides and props
- recounting story of someone's conversion
- reference to drama and song(s)
- personal application.

A look at the Seeker Service content and context is not to assume that the North American model is an appropriate one to transfer 'off the peg' into another cultural setting.

> It is in essence about how we allow the Willow Creek principles and process to assist us in creating events for seekers which are viable and effective in our particular cultural context.

In a way that's what makes it hard to write about. The context of a church set in the comfortable commuter suburbs will obviously be vastly different to a church set in a down-town urban context. That said, there is a value, I believe, in looking generally at some of the areas that need attention in setting up the seeker-event to enable the reader to benefit from the principles and processes which really work.

The Buildings

Much church 'plant' was built at a time when the religious and social constitution of society was markedly different. Though there was a time when it might have been reasonable to claim that Christianity was dominant in English society and that the buildings we have reflect that dominance, today it would be difficult

The Seeker Service 103

to maintain that Christianity is now such a force. In consequence, a lot of the buildings we have, though very beautiful, are uncomfortable places for many. Those of us who are familiar with church buildings appreciate what they communicate about the beauty and power of God. To many they communicate disease. Their sheer size tower over the uninitiated in judgement. Often they exude a coldness far more ominous than that of the air temperature to those who on occasion visit them.

On the other hand, a trip into modern cities affords a valuable insight into the way things have changed. A visit to the top of one of the many skyscrapers which constitute the skylines of our modern cities is revealing. Way below, the towers and spires of churches are dwarfed by these vast monuments to secularism. Of course, it is salutary to remember that there was a time when those churches dominated the landscape, themselves dwarfing the surrounding buildings. Sadly, many of those buildings today stand dirty and decaying, whilst the vast and glittering edifices of glass and concrete dominate. It is, in its way, a powerful testimony to the way society has changed not least in relation to the way that the Church has been both dwarfed and marginalised by the secular world.

Different people then, view church buildings with a mixture of differing attitudes. To those who cherish the Christian heritage of our land, our churches are places to be conserved, often irrespective of cost. To others churches are viewed with indifference, whilst for some they are objects of irritation, speaking about an institution of wealth that has played it's part in the past in the oppression of people. For many they are purely objects of convenience—always available as a stage-set for important family occasions, but largely to be avoided at other times.

Many of us feel the burden of large and expensive-to-maintain buildings. Yet, whether we like it or not, they are there. The growth of services in community buildings seems to indicate that for a good many people such buildings are eminently more accessible than more traditional church buildings. True, most people wouldn't want to get married or have their funeral conducted in a school hall or a library, but it may be that when it comes to regular worship such buildings have an edge. It does seen that talk of 'the symbolic value of church buildings', so popular with many Christians (not least clergy), is of limited impact when many people no longer relate to the meaning of that symbolism. The idea that proper worship can only take place in a church building is surely nonsense!

The building at Willow Creek is totally free of any religious symbolism. The feel of the 'church' (normally referred to as the 'auditorium') is much more akin to a large theatre or concert hall. When filled to capacity it will hold around 4,500 people. At the front is a large stage which is the focus of the activity, whether it's a seeker service or a believers service. The seating is fixed, more like comfortable cinema seating than church furniture. The foyer is large and the recently added 'atrium' is a huge space where people can meet to have a meal or a drink, or simply to talk. Everything about the building has been carefully thought through to make the environment as welcoming and undemanding as possible. The effect is very powerful.

The fact is that such luxury will be beyond most of the people reading this book. However, to start to think about the buildings we have in terms of their user-friendliness is a worthwhile exercise. Even small changes can make a big difference. The lighting we use can make a huge difference to the ambience of the building. Warmth and comfort are areas that can be addressed. A lavatory is fundamental, but sometimes not easy to site, especially if you are the custodian of a listed building! Many churches have spent large sums of money on re-ordering schemes. Though it would be difficult to argue that all such schemes have made an older building more seeker-friendly it is fair to say that a number of such schemes certainly have. The possibilities and examples are numerous.

Personally, I would generally favour the use of existing community buildings for seeker-targeted events. Unchurched people are usually more at ease in them. They are familiar places. The space available is usually flexible in the way that it can be used. They are free from the symbolism that can be so meaningless to unchurched people. They can be rented rather than owned – a big advantage when cash is scarce.

Facilities

Two further things to think about. Firstly, the better the facilities for childcare the more this will add to your seeker-friendliness. Most couples these days do not like the idea of leaving their new 'little bundle' in a creche where the floor is unkempt and the toys have been chewed by generations of children. Allied to this, but not immediately relevant to the building, is the fact that the people charged with looking after the young ones ought to instill confidence in those who bring their children along. There seems little point in providing poor childcare. If parents are sitting in church worrying about the child they have just left in the creche then the whole thing is counter-productive. What would it take for parents to leave their children in our care for over an hour with confidence? That may be a useful opening question for churches.

I well remember a church service which attracted a lot of interest and had frequent newcomers at the morning service. There was however a large 'bleed' rate, with many people coming for a short while and then disappearing. When some research was done as to why this was, it was discovered that a strong contributory factor was the poor level of childcare on offer.

Appearances

Secondly, if you're going to have a church noticeboard why not make it look good and communicate relevant and up-to-date information. A dejected Minister told me that he had been in his post for about two years when someone phoned him with a simple query. He was somewhat taken aback to be addressed by his predecessor's name. When the Minister pointed out that it was two and a half years since his predecessor had left, the caller apologised explaining that he had 'got the name from the church notice-board.' When you think about the time and money that the world invests in its attempts to communicate, it is somewhat humbling. Again, it's the issue of the signals you send.

First Impressions

As a younger man I loved amateur dramatics. At each performance at the theatre the audience was looked after by a very important person. His job title was 'Front of House Manager'. Though not directly involved with production his role was crucial. It was his task to get the people into the theatre and to their seats with the minimum of fuss; he, with his team of volunteers, would deal with any queries from the audience about the facility; should any problems arise he would handle them. No performance would begin without the Front of House Manager giving the signal.

It seems to me that this 'front-of-house ministry' is really important. In today's world people seem to be very affected by their first impressions. They will make an early decision about our churches on the basis of those first impressions, whether we like it or not. I know that many churches now give this part of their ministry a high priority. Training is often given so that those responsible recognise the importance of their role and also are equipped to carry it out. I feel certain that there are people who are gifted by God to undertake this ministry and in our churches we need to find these people and train them for this vital ministry, which is part of the 'welcome ministry'.

The Welcome Ministry

Not long ago I went to an evangelistic presentation where a large and well known church had sent a 'faith-sharing' team. Mostly, the people present gave the impression, by their familiarity with the songs that were sung, that they were already Christians. The first thing I noticed was that there was no one on the door. No one to welcome or to show visitors to their seats. There was no one there to give out the appropriate books or service sheets. Subsequently, I discovered that there was a pile of service sheets on a chair by the door, and that I had missed them. When the service began there was chaos as it was discovered that no one had the booklet that the person leading the worship assumed everybody had! An embarrassing interlude followed as people tried their best to get the booklets handed out as quickly as possible. What seems so tragic is that just a little more thought and planning could have made a huge difference to the service.

Again, a neighbouring church used to follow the excellent practice of printing the whole service on one sheet of paper. On the whole and where possible I would favour this every time. It just makes newcomers that bit more aware and therefore more relaxed. The problem was that in this particular church, the first two minutes of every service were taken up with the minister correcting all the mistakes on the service sheet. Again, I make the point that very little more care in the production of the sheet would have made a big difference.

These examples simply serve to 'flag the point' that it would not be difficult to make these small changes that would make a big difference. This front-of-house and welcome ministry is very important. Indeed it is not just important for special events, but for **all** our services. It's the difference between people being made to feel comfortable with what is going on rather than awkward and embarrassed.

At Willow Creek this ministry is taken with the utmost seriousness. From the moment someone arrives at Willow Creek till the moment they leave the emphasis is upon making them feel at ease. Car park attendants help deal with the traffic flow; ushers deal with this front-of-house ministry. They have received training on how much of a welcome to give. A lot of unchurched people find that an over-effusive and exaggerated welcome is threatening. Many people just want to come and go without a huge fuss being made. They have been taught that eye-contact is important when greeting someone. The task of making people feel welcome without making them feel threatened is a delicate balance to achieve.

Hybels himself talks about the need for anonymity. For people who have 'bucked up the courage' to attend, with or without a friend, it is important to recognise their need for anonymity. To be able to come and go without being hugged, or without someone trying to extract a name and address from newcomers is important.

Keeping in touch

I know a lot of Ministers, myself included, who have a highly developed (and mostly misguided) strategy for approaching newcomers. For a long time when someone new came to one of our services, my staff and I would extract a name and address from them. This was then followed up as quickly as possible with a visit to the house, often the next day. Though I feel embarrassed to admit it, my purpose could be described this way:

(a) To discover what they thought about the service.
(b) To apologise to them if they didn't like it. ('We're not usually as formal/informal as that.')
(c) To try and persuade them that people like me and my staff were exactly the kind of people in whose care their spiritual journey could be entrusted.
(d) To 'see off' any opposition. ('Oh you tried St Olave's Church. It's great there I'm told—if you like a formal and liberal church.')

(e) To sow a few seeds of guilt if they didn't return to our Church.

The subliminal message sent in this visit was something like this: 'You came to our Church.' Love–fifteen. 'I've come to your house.' Fifteen all. Now the ball is in your court.

Let me stress that this strategy was not something that I consciously articulated to myself or to any of the Church's staff. If you had accused me of some of these less-than-worthy motives I would have hotly denied it! On reflection all this is terrible from a number of angles. But out there somewhere are Ministers who know that they are doing exactly the same kind of thing – some of them have talked to me about it. What I came to see was that if we were offering the right kind of services for the right kind of people, then those same people would come back of their own volition. Things changed a lot for me in that discovery.

Respecting personal space

The point about autonomy is that it allows people the space to make up their own minds without inducing anxiety or guilt. The atmosphere to aim at, I believe, is one where newcomers are given the impression that if they wanted to talk, then the welcome team would talk to them. On the other hand it needs to be clear that if people don't want to talk – just to slip in and out – then that is equally acceptable. Probably in our culture in the UK, I would hesitate to have the welcome team show people to their seats. Maybe it's better to be self-levelling in this, allowing people to sit where they feel most comfortable. Usually they don't march straight to the front seats!

The Seeker Service 111

The need to hold something in the hands

Another feature that needs careful attention, as I implied earlier in the chapter, is the whole area of the resources that we hand to people for the service. At one extreme it's giving people four or five books and sheets of paper to find their way around; at the other extreme it's giving people nothing because, 'all you need will be on the overhead'. Probably the first is less seeker-friendly than the second, but both are uncomfortable for the unchurched. Certainly people don't want to be made to look stupid by not being able to find their way around books they haven't seen before. Let's face it, some of us use some pretty thick books! Even when Ministers give page numbers (and lots don't), newcomers find it difficult to respond. The alternative of having nothing but the overhead projector assumes at least two things: (a) They can see over a distance, and (b) They will be comfortable with nothing in their hands.

Neither of these assumptions seems to be likely. The first is obviously a very dubious assumption. The second one is more interesting. In a situation where people may be feeling self-conscious some will worry about 'what to do with my hands'. At least a book or a service sheet gives you something to hold. Those churches which favour the overhead alone do so on the historical basis that it frees you to do other things such as wave your arms in the air or 'dance before the Lord'. A good many unchurched people are terrified by such behaviour! I do think, however, that the overhead is excellent for use where children are present, especially if they sit together at the front.

Be informative

My preferred option would always be the printed service sheet with everything on it. If you can't fit it all on two sides of an A4 sheet (folded) then the chances are that the service will not be seeker-friendly on the grounds of length! A sheet gives people something in their hands and allows easy access to the content of the service for newcomers. It should also tell them what's on the 'menu' even when the emphasis is on presentation rather than participation. True, a service sheet is expensive and generates more work to produce, but I believe it to be a sound investment of time and money. The growth in the use of PC's with word processing packages means that most congregations would be able to find the resources to produce a professional and attractive sheet. The cost of such an investment would be an act of faith for some congregations – but isn't that what we're about?

Allowing for literacy needs

Where there is a literacy problem in the congregation it is probably better to major on presentation anyway. Such a context provides a challenge to many of the wordy services which many of us appear to favour. To totally ignore literacy as an issue is to send a signal about the kind of people we expect to see in our churches.

Choice of personnel

I believe this front-of-house ministry is important and that many of us could improve our accessibility to the unchurched by giving more attention to it. Perhaps someone in our church should be given this area of ministry to organise as a specific task. At any event, the more we can do to make people feel comfortable with the environment the better. But it does involve thinking outside our normal frame of reference and sphere of operation by putting ourselves in the place of the unchurched seeker.

The Music Ministry

A good many unchurched people cannot easily relate to the music we who are Christians love and are familiar with. Some of the research that Willow Creek did in the early years revealed that one of the principle reasons that people did not attend a church was that they were unable to relate to the music. A lot of church music is an acquired taste and most people who don't come to church haven't acquired it. There is no 'right' music for use in churches. What is right is the kind of music that people in a particular context can relate to.

In saying this I do not envisage that traditional church music will be redundant in seeker churches. It will however need to be heavily supplemented by music which will be more readily accessible to the unchurched. Most people do not have experience of either classical or more traditional choral music and, in consequence do not readily relate to it when confronted by it. In some ways it simply re-inforces in the minds of the unchurched that the church is out-moded and out-of-date.

Of course, there are huge problems here. Many church musicians are openly resistant to contemporary music. Indeed, to hear some of them talk you would think that the presence and use of a church organ was some kind of divine ordinance! If we are serious about reaching the unchurched then we have to be prepared to choose and to use music from a much broader base than the material we use at present. At Willow Creek the musicians talk about and model a 'servant' attitude in their approach to their ministry, which many of us could certainly learn from. Their passion is to serve the goal of reaching lost people for Christ. Because of that they are willing to play what they are requested to play.

Neither is this a plea for us simply to slip into the current vogue in worship of services where modern choruses are sung repetitively. My guess is that quite a number of these modern choruses are as difficult for the unchurched to relate to as more traditional church music. It may well be that we have to begin to look at some contemporary secular music, much of it expressing a deep and radical questioning of the world in which we live, some of it surpassing modern Christian music in terms of both depth and quality.

The need for song writers

Again, part of the problem is that we need Christian composers who share a vision for reaching the unchurched who can write music which is relevant both in terms of idiom and lyrics. I think I have learnt relatively late in my life that the potential of music for reaching unchurched people for Christ is huge. The right music, used creatively is a powerful tool in opening the hearts and minds of unchurched people. This is not to say that we should use music to manipulate emotionally those who come to our churches. More simply it is a recognition that music can sometimes reach those parts that some sermons will never reach! Of course there will always be people who will be deeply moved by a performance of Handel's 'Messiah'. At the same time there are many people whose musical background will mean that such music will, by and large, leave them cold.

The need for a broad repertoire

At Willow Creek the music is a very strong area of ministry. Of course today from the resource base from which they operate, they are able to produce music of the highest quality in just about every style from classical to rock and roll. The important thing is that they do just that. The balance of music used would be weighted towards contemporary music, but used creatively and with a mixture of different styles. Most people who visit Willow Creek are struck by the quality of the music. They seem to be skilled in creating the 'emotional moment' without the manipulation which so often lurks in the background on other occasions. Many people are challenged again to look at the music ministry in their own churches.

The need for a flexible music group

Though the now mandatory music group has uneasily become a part of the fabric in many churches, such groups tend to be understandably pre-occupied with producing Christian music for worship. However limited this is for reaching the unchurched it is a step in the right direction. In a recent article, Tim Thornborough in a somewhat lighthearted way reflected on what was attractive in a charismatic community church which he had paid a visit to. Writing under the heading of 'music' he writes:

> A good modern band (not too loud) played the music in a contemporary way. Although one of my past criticisms of 'charismatic' choruses has been that they are simple and repetitive, I had not before recognised that this makes them easy to learn and sing for the newcomer and the non-musical.[1]

It does seem that the whole area of music will make a large difference to the cutting-edge of our churches. Congregations which persist in a narrow diet of music which is of minority interest are likely to be the churches which produce narrow and minority congregations. Those churches which experiment with music are to be encouraged in their endeavours.

Drama and Dance

Many churches have already discovered the potential of getting across the message by using the creative arts. Over the years drama groups have enriched the life and mission of the church. In some ways the potential is unlimited. I confess that once or twice in my preaching ministry a drama performed prior to a talk has been so powerful in it's impact that I had almost wished the service could end on that note. The talk to follow seemed almost superfluous.

Drama has certainly figured large in Willow Creek's ministry. I have never attended a seeker service at which there has not been a dramatic presentation. The sheer quality of the dramas I have seen there has at times been awesome. The way in which humour and other human emotions have been touched by the dramas has provided an excellent platform upon which the message has been preached. Indeed the way drama appears to be used in Willow Creek is to provide a basis for the preaching of the message. Often the drama asks questions rather than provides answers.

The need for script writers

Willow Creek write most of their own scripts, some of which are now available for purchase outside the USA. Already churches which are trying to do seeker services are writing their own scripts. My guess is that within a very short time those churches which would not feel able to provide their own scripts will be able to avail themselves of scripts that have been written in other churches. The scripts from Willow Creek work well with minor adaptation outside America—at least that's what the practitioners tell me.

I always feel that drama is something that we don't exploit enough in our churches. Most congregations whatever their size can usually identify some people who are gifted in this area. Workshops for those interested are on the increase so that adequate and relatively cheap training can be provided. Scripts for use in a variety of contexts can be easily obtained. Indeed a lot of our worship could be greatly enriched by the more creative use of drama. There's something about the visual aspects of a drama which is very engaging, not least in a world where much of what people learn comes via the television—a visual experience.

The need for rehearsal

Of course, if done poorly a drama can have the opposite effect. In a seeker context, one of the worst things we can do to unchurched people is to embarrass them. The old worldly saying that, 'if a thing is worth doing, it's worth doing well' has a relevance here. Lines need to be learnt rather than read from a scrappy piece of paper. Rehearsal is vital with some proper production prior to performance.

The need to make dance relevant

The issue of dance in worship is one that I have a certain ambivalence about. As I have friends whose wives are professional dancers, I am still willing to be persuaded about the seeker potential of dance. My natural inclination is to be wary. This is partly based in my own experience as most of the dance that I have seen performed in churches has embarrassed me. My suspicion is that it has at times embarrassed others as well. Strangely, this is not necessarily a comment on the quality. Indeed, as far as I know, some of the dances that have embarrassed me have been performed very capably. I find it difficult to articulate as to why this is. The one dance that I did think was impressive in a seeker context was performed by a male dancer whose dance was somewhere between a kung-fu demonstration and gymnastics. This said, I'm sure that dance has some possibilities. Perhaps I've just been unfortunate thus far!

I think that part of my unease is to do with the fact that quite a lot of the dance that I have observed has been performed by amateurs. I'm not sure that dance for use in a public context can be done by untrained people with just a couple of hours practice beforehand. The other thing that is important is that a dance for the sake of a dance is probably not good enough. It needs to be tied to the theme of the service and help people interpret that theme in new ways. Above all I think that dance needs to be theatrical. I suspect that mime is a medium which is well worth exploring. Some of the most powerful presentations I have seen involved mime, combining the movement of dance with theatre.

In seeker services there is real scope for the use of the creative arts. Of course none of this is new and several churches have for years been seeking to creatively use the arts as a tool of mission. What is different in the seeker context is that their use is strongly tailored to the cultural context of the people to be reached, rather than being used to fit in with 'church culture'. I think that statement relates to my unease with most of the dance I have seen performed in churches.

Preaching at Seeker Services

Absolutely central to the seeker service is the message that is preached. On the whole I think that it is preachers who build churches. A lot of what happens at seeker services is to provide a platform for the preaching of the message. In some ways it would be possible to produce a whole book on the subject because of its importance and because there is a need to look again at this vital area.

The principle point to make on this subject is that a lot of preaching with an evangelistic slant misses its mark because its starting point is a long way away from where a lot of people in secular culture are. For a start, without trying, most of us preachers can slip into the jargon of our faith. The formal context of a lot of preaching can in itself provide a barrier.

Ed Dobson in his book *Starting a Seeker Service* writes the following:

> I have worked hard at the delivery of the talk without preaching. First, I dress in casual clothes such as blue jeans and a T-shirt to invite a relaxed, informal atmosphere. Second, I sit on a bar stool and use a hand-held microphone. When I walk around as I talk, I tend to get 'preachy'. Sitting down, I tend to be more conversational in style.[2]

I would suggest that Ed Dobson has discovered an informal way of preaching for himself which sounds nearer the mark than the way many of us were taught to preach. Not that I am suggesting that we all don jeans and T-shirts to preach. What I am saying is that in our own context we need to ask questions about how we might make our delivery a little more informal and in consequence a little more accessible.

What kind of things should we be preaching about? It's here that there will be controversy in the approach that is needed. We need to be preaching biblically on subjects that are of relevance to our hearers. That is to say, not subjects that we perceive to be relevant, but subjects that the hearers themselves can identify as relevant to their lives. Just because a preacher tells a congregation that something is relevant doesn't mean that his hearers will perceive it to be so.

The limitation of expositional preaching

Though I firmly believe that expository preaching is vital in building up the Church, I do not believe that this is the right tool for reaching the unchurched. James M. Gordon, attempting to analyse John Stott's thinking, wrote that 'the Christian mind does not think exclusively about "Christian" topics but thinks about every topic "Christianly".[3] It is this way of thinking, in my opinion, that needs to infect our preaching to the unchurched.

For many people today the case for the use of Scripture needs to be made before people will be willing to use it as a basis from which to order their lives. They need to be able to see that there is a relevance. Of course there are around a very few extremely gifted expository preachers and it would be folly to claim that they do not see genuine growth in their churches. There is still a question as to whether this is the right model for preaching in an age which has by and large rejected books as a basis of gaining knowledge and in which there appears to be so few gifted expositors. I heard some while ago a tape by the excellent American Bible expositor John McArthur in which he was lamenting the loss of a book culture and with it the loss of peoples' ability to think analytically. Such a cultural gap makes the expositor's task all the more difficult.

Most of the people who are in the business of trying to reach the unchurched are realising that they are having to learn new skills in this area. That they cannot take anything for granted in preaching to these people. Ed Dobson makes the point well:

> John R. Stott offers an excellent model of preaching in his book, *Between Two Worlds*. He states that preaching begins in the world of biblical truth and builds a bridge into the world of everyday living. This is the approach I use at Sunday Services: I usually teach from the Bible verse by

> verse, then I try to apply the truth in practical ways to my life and the lives of the congregation. However, I do not use that model at 'Saturday Night' [i.e. his seeker service]. Instead, I do the reverse: I begin in the real world of everyday life, and I stay in that world for most of the talk. Eventually I turn to the world of biblical truth to demonstrate that the Bible is relevant for today.[4]

How long should you preach to the unchurched for? Most of us would be tempted to preach for as short a time as possible. Were we to adopt a more traditional model of preaching that would be a reasonable basis. However, a good number of those who have experience in preaching to the unchurched tend to speak for over twenty minutes. Hybels would normally preach for up to half an hour. Some seeker church preachers follow their talk with a Question and Answer session inviting and getting a response from the hearers to their message. This is something that is worth looking at. On occasions it may well be worth interviewing someone about their Christian faith. This can be a powerful and less threatening way for people to see how Christianity can impact people's lives.

Popular topics

The choice of topic is crucial. Topics that have an obvious relevance to the lives of ordinary people are vital. Again, the perception of many people, even the faithful, is that they cannot relate to the message. Most seeker churches seem to opt for a blend of issues related to everyday living and issues related to Christian apologetics. A typical example of the kind of things that would be appropriate would be as follows:

Facing Life's Challenges

Week 1 'Coping with my stress'
Week 2 'Coping with my fear'
Week 3 'Coping with my anger'
Week 4 'Coping with my disappointments'
Week 5 'Coping with my loneliness'
Week 6 'Coping with my death'

This six-week course is intended as an example of teaching aimed at the experience of ordinary people. Not that everyone is facing all these issues at the same time, rather that these are the kinds of things that we all face at one time or another. The next example is the kind of more apologetic-based preaching.

Testing Questions

Week 1 'Why does God allow suffering?'
Week 2 'Science and Religion – Worlds Apart?'
Week 3 'Is the Bible really true?'
Week 4 'Aren't all religions really the same?'
Week 5 'Can someone who's dead come back to life?'
Week 6 'Isn't religion just for weak people?'

With imagination there are many more subjects and some excellent fun titles to be created. One course of sermons I saw was called 'Turning life's bitter lemons into lemonade!'

Let it be said that preaching in this way mostly demands an awful lot of preparation. It's vital that it is understood that if you are preaching to seekers that you have some kind of handle on their world. To put it bluntly it's no good quoting from *The Times* newspaper if most of your hearers take the *Sun*. I believe that preaching to seekers is extremely exciting. I also believe that it is extremely demanding. It will mean that we shall not only need to be competent in our handling of our biblical theology, but we shall also need to be informed about the world of our hearers. This may take us to newspapers and periodicals, or the cinema or even to the television to watch the 'soaps'.

Using visual aids

Anecdotes and stories are fine providing they are not too abstract, they are relevant to what you want to talk about, and they do not over-proliferate. Visual aids can be useful. It has always seemed strange to me that in church culture we largely assume that visual aids are only appropriate when children are present. My experience has always been that a good many adults get more from family service talks than from talks aimed at adults. Those churches which have extensive resources will avail themselves of the more expensive high-tech video projectors which open up a whole new world for the communicator. If we are to use visual aids in this context it is vital that they are of reasonable quality. Many preachers do not have a giftedness in producing visual aids. There may well, however, be someone in the congregation for whom this will become their primary ministry.

Programming

It is well worth appointing someone who will coordinate the whole seeker presentation. In Willow Creek this activity is called programming. The work of the person responsible for programming is to take the theme for the service and 'programme' the music, drama, testimony, etc., to fit in with the theme. They have the final say as to what runs and what doesn't.

The person responsible for programming will meet before the service with those who are responsible for producing the various parts of the presentation. At that meeting the theme will be discussed and initial ideas will be put on the table until a framework is established. Further work will then be done on the constituent parts before the whole is brought together for a final run through. The person responsible for programming will have an eye on the time. It seems likely that an hour is the maximum time for a seeker service.

It is largely because what goes on at a seeker service is fashioned to connect with the culture of those that have been targeted that the event is very often alarming for Christians used to worship services. Even talk of 'targeting' groups of people will no doubt attract criticism. The sad thing is, that without using such language many congregations have effectively been targeting a small group of people for a very long time and largely inadvertently.

Notes

1. Article entitled 'I'm a pair of Kippers for the Lord' by Tim Thornborough in *The Briefing* edition no. #121 published by St. Matthias Press.
2. *Starting a Seeker-Sensitive Service* by Ed Dobson, Scripture Press (1994), p. 50.
3. *Evangelical Spirituality–from the Wesleys to John Stott*, James M. Gordon, SPCK (1991), p. 29.
4. *Starting a Seeker-Sensitive Service* by Ed Dobson, Scripture Press (1994), p. 48.

7

Re-ordering the Church for Mission

As has been mentioned, the move from a maintenance model to a missionary model of church is a shift that will demand a massive commitment of careful, prayerful and godly leadership. In most churches the values and structures upon which our churches have been built have assumed a maintenance mode. But what kind of values and structures will be required if our churches are to be rebuilt on different foundations? It is worth restating that without this change any new methods or techniques will quickly prove useless. These values need to be owned by as many of our membership as is possible at any one time.

What principles will need to be articulated if these values are to become the norm? Whatever these principles are they will never be substitutes for Spirit-empowered, prayerful Christianity. Without the assistance of the Holy Spirit and a dependence upon God expressed through prayer our efforts will be largely in vain. This point cannot be overstressed. These principles are certainly not new. Indeed they have their basis in the Bible and that's why they are very important.

Before referring to these principles there's something else to be aware of. The call to be a missionary church is not a call to a shallow, flippant, 'bubble-gum' Christianity. There is much today in churches which smacks of superficiality. It is likely that where such a shallow spirituality exists the church's mission will be limited. It's not that there is an element of choice about this—as though we could opt in our churches for either a deep and rich spirituality or a popular missionary appeal to the unchurched. It's not an either/or option. The two go together.

It might well be asked how we might recognise a church with a genuine and authentic spirituality. My answer to that question would lay great store on the fruits of the Holy Spirit. I would expect that in a church which had a genuine and deep spirituality there would be, in the lives of the faithful, a harvest of Christ-like qualities. Galatians 5 tells us that this harvest of the Spirit includes these qualities: love, joy, peace, patience, kindness, goodness, faithfulness, gentleness and self-control.

There may be all kinds of false piety around, but the fruit of the Spirit is not easily mimicked—at least not for long. Clearly, where there is hatred, anger, intolerance, gossip and envy in a church (and it happens!) there must be a shadow over the spirituality of that church. It is certainly fair to say that where these fruits of the Spirit are lacking, the missionary task of the church will be seriously undermined. In a world crying out for love and acceptance, a church which offers the opposite is unlikely to be of appeal. Obviously, if we wait till the Church is perfect then we shall never begin our missionary task. God knows that we'll make our mistakes and that in most of us His Spirit will take time to erode the rough edges of our personalities. Thankfully His forgiveness awaits those who acknowledge their mistakes and turn to Him afresh.

Principles of Mission

Let me share some of these principles in the hope that as you take them to heart the Holy Spirit will begin His work of renewing the mind of His Church.

What kind of principles will churches in 'missionary' mode espouse?

1. Churches which make a priority of mission

This is all very obvious. However it needs to be articulated time and time again. We reveal our priorities by the way we behave. The starting point for many of us will be to recognise that mission has not been our priority. Indeed, by the way we have modelled our churches it is doubtful whether it would be obvious that it was even on the agenda in many cases. It is worth reflecting that this message will not just be received through teaching. It will require those in leadership not only to talk about mission but to do mission. If church leaders don't hang out with the unchurched then church members will quickly conclude that it doesn't really matter if they don't. Someone who had just returned from Willow Creek said to me that one of the impressive things about Bill Hybels was that he still made a priority of spending time with unbelievers, modelling in his own life the message that he wanted to teach the church.

It may well be worth asking our church organisations to review their activities in the light of their missionary potential. How might they reorganise themselves to ensure that mission was a visible priority in their ministry? What should we do with various sub-ministries which seem to have passed their 'sell-by date' in terms of their mission potential? Just to ask these questions does two things. Firstly, it sends a signal about prioritising mission; secondly, from such fundamental questioning new life can be breathed into existing ministries.

2. Churches which understand that all *their members are missionaries*

This cannot be overstressed. The scenario is easily recognisable. If you ask the question, 'Who are your missionaries?' you will usually be shown the church notice board on which are photographs of those who have responded to the call to serve Christ as missionaries overseas. It's those people who many church members regard as **the** missionaries. Of course such people are missionaries and their calling is absolutely valid. My point is that mission is the task of the whole church and not just those who serve God overseas.

Regrettably such a limited view is neither adequate nor biblical. In Acts 1 Jesus tells his disciples that they are all to be his witnesses. This doesn't mean that all his followers will have the specialist gift of evangelism. But it does mean that all have their part to play in the missionary task of the Church. This will be based not just on the things we say, but on the way our lives, corporately as a church, and also as individuals, model those Kingdom qualities that Christ is seeking in us.

This is an attitude that will take time to nurture in

our congregations. The culture of churches doesn't change overnight. To use the current jargon the issue is about empowering the church to be the church. Giving back to all members their God-given responsibility for mission. Such empowerment restores dignity to the Body. A dignity that the Church badly needs.

3. Churches which understand the need to relate what they do on Sunday to what their members are doing for the other six days of the week

There's a lot that could be said about this. A friend of mine speaks helpfully of the distinction he makes between the church in what he calls the 'gathered mode', i.e. at worship or prayer meetings, etc., and the church in 'dispersed mode', i.e. when Christians are at work or in their homes or schools, etc. A clarifying question is how the church in gathered mode is equipping its members for when they are in dispersed mode.

In other words there should be a relationship between the two modes. For a lot of people it is making this connection that is a real problem. In consequence, their Christianity is something they can only make sense of when they are within the 'safety zone' of the church in its gathered mode. A church seeking to prioritise for mission will be seeking to help people make these connections for themselves.

4. Churches which understand that the Incarnation is the crucial model for Mission

The Church's repository of teaching is rich with books and papers on this particular topic. However it is always worth re-visiting this fundamental truth. For God's motivation in sending His Son to us is clear.

'God so loved the world that He gave...' It is because of God's love that Jesus came. Here is a salutary reminder that our motive in mission should be love. Our concern for mission should not stem from a desire to generate more money or to be part of a big set-up, but rather should come from our love for the lost. Why? Because those peoples are important to God. If this is true then some important foundational principles flow from this basic truth:

(a) The starting point for many will need to be a release of the Holy Spirit's power within us to rekindle a love for lost people.
(b) If love is our motivation we shall focus on mission conducted in and through relationships.
(c) Just as love demands sacrifice, so mission which is motivated by love will be costly to those who participate.
(d) Mission motivated by love will never be manipulative or coercive, but will 'treat people with gentleness and respect' (1 Peter 3:15).

5. Churches which understand the need to engage with culture

Part of the insight that the Incarnation brings with it bears strongly on this matter of culture. For in choosing to send His Son to humanity, God in some senses entered a particular culture at a particular point in time. The demands of mission motivated by love will mean that we shall need to ask ourselves what we shall need to become in order to love others. Clearly this has major cultural ramifications. One has only to start to think about the Church and young people to see the vast scope of the problem.

Re-ordering the Church for Mission

6. Churches which understand that taking risks is OK

One characteristic which seems to prevail in our churches is a strong desire to live within the safety zones of our own comfort level. The consequence being that a lot of what we do in our churches seems to have a high degree of safety about it. I do believe that mission today will demand us taking a few risks in our efforts to take the Gospel of Jesus Christ to the unchurched around us. We may have to try a few things that don't work; experiment with some imaginative ideas that might seem strange to our regular members. The business of engaging with culture is in itself risky.

In a book which made a big impact on me many years ago, *Dare to Live Now*, Bruce Larson ended a chapter, in which he had highlighted the need for us to understand that faith involves a degree of risk, by quoting Nicholas Murray Butler who said,

> I divide the world into three classes – the few who make things happen; the many who watch things happen; and the overwhelming majority who have no notion of what happens. We all want to belong to that class of people who 'make things happen'. There is a desperate need today for people of Christian faith – people who will make things happen by God's power, according to His will.[1]

To those words and particular in the context of the Church's mission I would add a loud, 'AMEN'.

Structures are Important

To teach these principles will not of necessity lead to a church which is mission-minded. We need to understand that the structures that we have, very often inhibit mission rather than encourage it. Again, this is primarily because those structures have been largely created to service the running of the church rather than assist us in the task of mission. Of course some of these existing structures will overlap with the task of mission. Worship, pastoral and outreach Committees may well be seeking to give a missionary focus to the church. There is much to be grateful for. Sadly many church structures, often those charged with executive responsibility, lose their nerve, and fashion albeit inadvertently, a maintenance mind-set. The question of what are appropriate structures in a church gearing for mission is important. This question will only be of relevance when we have designated our priorities.

Structures relating to the way finance is both raised and administered are usually crucial. Clearly in many churches this is where real power is held! It may be a helpful exercise to categorise the church's financial decisions over the last two years under the headings of 'maintenance' and 'mission', to get some kind of feel for where the church is.

Skilful analysis

It might be well worth a church inviting someone to undertake an audit of its resources and structures. Our churches have many people whose commercial background would enable them to give some consultancy on the efficacy and efficiency of our activities in relation to mission. No doubt they would be well able to offer some recommendations about how these could be restructured to facilitate the church in its missionary task. A SWOT analysis could be performed to assess Strengths, Weaknesses, Opportunities and Threats.

The Needs of Believers and the Needs of Seekers

At some stage fairly early on, the church will have to make a fundamental decision.

> Can the church meet the need of both seekers and believers in one act of worship?

Many churches will be happy to answer in the affirmative. It is perfectly possible to devise worship in which both needs are met. A good example has been the Family Service which has been largely a success. Without targeting strongly any group within the congregation the sheer accessibility of the service has meant that it has provided much needed growth in many churches. Whether the movement to a weekly service of Holy Communion in many churches, has helped the missionary cutting edge of the Church is, at best, debatable.

A look at the Anglican Church in England, where the 'parish communion' has been dominant, offers little encouragement. As the move to parish communion has gathered momentum in the church, the number of people attending Anglican churches has fallen. Between 1979 and 1989 the attendance at Anglican Church Services fell by nine per cent. Though it would be preposterous to lay the whole blame for that on churches which had opted for a parish communion, the facts certainly bear careful scrutiny. Many of my friends argue passionately that the parish communion is 'the way forward'. I still need a lot of persuasion! Christ's instruction to 'do this in remembrance of me' was addressed to believers.

Of course the issue is not just for churches which have a parish communion. This book has already alluded to the fact that lively, charismatic worship can be equally alienating for the unchurched.

> **So far the bold strategy is to concede that to try and meet the needs of both Christians and the unchurched in one act of worship is folly. It runs the risk of having little attraction to both groups.**

I think one of the most daring and fundamental decisions that Willow Creek took was to go for seeker services and worship services at different times. I heard recently from a colleague of a rural church in the UK which has been holding a monthly seeker service. The attendance at that service was 170 of which one third of the attenders were previously unchurched. This compared with an average attendance of 50 at their regular service. This must say something!

The issue of re-ordering our churches' structures for mission needs careful attention. Again, the danger of rushing into seeker-services cannot be overstressed. Personally, I would like to see every church in the country appoint someone who would give them consultancy on their mission strategy. Their role would be to give objective counsel on strategy and structures, as well as help churches sit down once in a while and review what they are doing.

Note

1. *Dare to live Now*, Bruce Larson, Zondervan (1965).

8

Small Beginnings

A good many people will be left with what is a very important question. How does all of this relate to the smaller church? Many churches throughout the world have a membership of 100 and smaller. Is the concept of the seeker church relevant only to the larger churches in the world? And what about those churches of any size which can't budget large sums of money for seeker services or produce endless supplies of human resources?

Well, it's challenging to think that when reading the teaching of Jesus there is a distinct emphasis upon small beginnings. I feel sure that when God looks at His Church He does not consider that only large churches are worthy of His blessing. To suggest otherwise would be tantamount to a blasphemy. We do well to remember that Jesus started a world-wide movement from the raw-material of twelve ordinary men.

Ed Dobson concludes in his chapter on *Seeker Services in a Smaller Setting* that:

> The answer lies in applying the principles of
> seeker ministry, not in imitating the details
> of a particular programme. Perhaps the most
> important principle is to relate the gospel in
> a culturally relevant way to unchurched
> people...[1]

The emphasis throughout this book has been on the importance of applying principles and process rather than merely copying a product. The first step for members of any church that wants to take a seeker ministry seriously will be to get in contact with the unchurched. This in itself would be indicative of a swing away from the ghetto mentality that pervades many churches. Many Christians, both in large and small churches have become isolated from the unchurched. Indeed, even more worrying, they have often become very uncomfortable with the kind of lifestyle of unchurched people and so have opted to keep away. They don't like smoking, or swearing, or drinking and they make it very obvious.

To illustrate their distaste of unchurched company Christians will often go to extraordinary lengths to keep away from them. They will create Christian versions of secular activities. I once played in a Christian Football League. Apart from the fact that it was difficult to see the difference between the Christian league and its more worldly counterparts—other than a slightly awkward gathering at the centre circle for prayers before the match began—the message that our Christian league sent to the others must have been very mixed. I applauded the church team which left our league and joined a 'normal' soccer league—not least when they achieved a good end-of-season league position. Surely sport is an excellent opportunity for us to get alongside the unchurched. The same could be said of many Christian activities. How much better when Christians get stuck in to organisations which are not based around the church. The opportunities are terrific.

When I went to a previous job, the membership of the church was minimal to say the least. I remember the tremendous pressure there was to start more and more church activities. In reality I came to see that what we needed was not to try and copy the activity base of larger churches, but to increase our contact with the thousands of unchurched people in the immediate vicinity. Of course hanging out with unchurched people may well attract the suspicion and even the hostility of other Christians who will be both challenged and threatened by what they will perceive to be worldliness. I reconcile all this by recalling the hostility that Jesus attracted from the Pharisees and the scribes for keeping company with those considered to be 'sinners'.

In some ways the smaller church is better placed to begin to face some of these crucial issues. Because they seldom have the resources to maintain a large menu of church activities they may well have more time to spend beyond the 'safety-zone' of the church. Dealing with issues like this which are quite threatening for most Christians can be often better handled in a small community. In larger groups it's easier to hide!

True, a regular seeker event will not be an easy option, though it may be possible to do such an event two or three times a year, especially if you pool resources with other churches. Giving special attention to the major Christian Festivals and seeing them as an opportunity for a seeker-sensitive approach is a good way to start.

Many churches are finding that a small group especially for people who are seeking or enquiring is an excellent way of following up a major festival service. To run one of these does not demand huge human resources and can, in different social contexts be an extremely effective tool. There are pre-prepared materials available to help the leaders of such groups, which can be adapted to fit your situation. In certain contexts a home will be an appropriate venue, in others a more public building. Some have even run this kind of group in a pub or school!

It is important for a small church to believe that with the help of God it can begin to grow. In some ways I think that such a belief is half the battle. It may well be that in a small church the teacher will have to spend more time nurturing a vision of growth. A vision which has manageable proportions and realistic goals. In my experience in a smaller church it's better to do a very limited amount well than a lot of things badly. Real discernment is needed to know where your resources will be best utilised. It is crucial in a church with limited resources to do several things:

(a) Nurture a vision for growth. Encourage members to believe that as we 'plant and water' so God will provide the growth (1 Corinthians 3:6-7). If small churches are to grow it is vital that members believe that growth is possible and desirable.
(b) Pray for God's strength and wisdom.
(c) Decide what your priorities are and don't expend resources and energy on non-priority activity.

Small Beginnings 143

(d) Looking at your list of priorities, pray about which one to start on.

(e) Try and give to God your best. Don't sacrifice quality for quantity!

(f) Discover whether there are any other Christian congregations with whom you could work in mission. What possibilities would open up if you pooled your resources? It seems more likely that God will bless a collaborative attitude rather than a competitive one.

Some Ideas for the Smaller Church

1. Run a course of sermons at all your Sunday Services on the theme of 'Mission and the Local Church'. Try and articulate the principles you see as important in seeing the shift away from maintenance to mission. It may be possible to enlist some help with this by inviting guest speakers.

2. A Parish Study Day could tackle a similar theme.

3. Initiate some discussions at your church council on any of the following subjects and give some quality agenda time to it.

   - What might we add to or subtract from our present services to make them more friendly for the unchurched?

   - How could we realistically alter our building to make it more welcoming?

   - What would we need to change in our church's timetable to encourage mission?

144 *Reaching the Unchurched*

- How could we discover what the wider community thinks about the local church?
- If we were starting a church from scratch what service pattern would we adopt? Any discussion topics which might facilitate some 'green-field' thinking would be excellent.

4. Start some prayer triplets which focus on praying for our unchurched friends or family.

5. Run one or two enquirer's groups annually at which Christianity is put under the spotlight.

6. A men's night or breakfast meeting with a speaker.*

7. A women's coffee, luncheon or evening meeting with a speaker.*

8. A 'couples' event with a speaker.*

9. The use of interview or testimony at Sunday Services.

10. Specify a week in the church's diary where members are encouraged to invite unchurched friends into their homes.* Obviously in certain social contexts this would not be appropriate.

11. A community survey to help our church understand better the facts about our locality.

12. Plan to make your Christmas and Easter services seeker events.*

13. Discover one community need you could meet and invent a creative way of meeting it.

14. Hold a parish party and ask each of your members

Small Beginnings   145

to bring an unchurched friend. Probably not an occasion for a speaker!*

15. Try and get two of your members to undertake some training in the important area of community care.

16. Hold some specialist, targeted services, e.g. for those bereaved over a period; for those who have cause to give thanks for recovery from illness; for those with pets to bless; for those who have been married for over 20 years, etc.*

17. Set up a 'Care Call' system where people who are ill or housebound receive a telephone call once per week.

18. Organise a Parish walk and encourage church members to bring unchurched friends.

19. Organise a children's holiday club during summer holidays which culminates in a seeker event for parents and children.*

20. Invite the Headteachers of local schools to your Church Councils to speak on how the church might best serve the local school.

21. Have a 'Welcome Pack' from the church which goes to people who move into the area. This pack would outline your activities and church programme. This can easily be done in co-operation with other local churches.

22. Teach regularly in church and in other teaching contexts on how church members can effectively, naturally and sensitively witness to their Christian faith.

23. Actively encourage your church members to belong to a community organisation in which they have an interest.

* Given that a church decides to plot some 'Enquirer's Groups', those ideas marked with an asterisk are occasions at which publicity for such groups could easily and naturally be handed out. Well produced, printed invitations to which a name, date, time and venue could be easily added would seem to be a sensible option.

It is clear that, in some senses the size of the church is not the issue that it may seem. For the working out of the principles can happen in any context. Size will, on the whole, only determine the scale of seeker-activity we can generate. In some ways I can see that smaller churches will find it easier to appropriate the principles and start work on the transformational agenda of moving to a mission mind-set.

A Tailor-made Strategy for Each Location

The ability to ask the right questions is as helpful, in many cases, as being able to give the right answers. Central to this book is the recognition that although Willow Creek may not have all the right answers (and, in fairness, would not claim to have them), they are certainly asking some big questions. It is important that some of the questions raised in this book are considered carefully before any strategy for mission is planned. For me a central question is, 'What kind of churches will we need to assist the process of turning people who are unchurched into fully devoted followers of Jesus Christ? The question, as has been noted, seems further complicated by the post-Christian culture in which the Church in many developed countries finds itself.

Has Willow Creek got anything to offer the rest of us? The answer is to be found in Australia, New Zealand, the UK and beyond. Churches seeking to implement their own seeker strategies are discovering that a kind of renewal is happening within congregations and growth is taking place. The Gospel is reaching the hearts of people who were previously untouched.

The 'Value-Added' Task

Of course, there are those who will be sceptical of a church which appears to be customer-driven. Such a judgement is, in my view mistaken. Willow Creek, I would argue is a 'value-driven' model of church. Working from a strong and somewhat simple mission statement, Willow Creek identify eight biblical values which 'drive' all they do as a Church. The Mission Statement and values are described below:

Mission Statement

> 'To turn irreligious people into fully devoted followers of Jesus Christ'

The Eight Biblical Values of Willow Creek Community Church

1. The Church is to operate as a Body

(1 Corinthians 12:4 and 13; Romans 12) Includes the concepts of spiritual giftedness, passion and personal

styles; ministry accomplished in teams, and diversity.

2. Full devotion to Christ is normal for a believer

(1 Kings 11:4; Philippians 2:1-11; 2 Corinthians 8:6,7) Includes the concepts of stewardship, servanthood and downward mobility (ministry over occupation).

3. Lost people matter to God, therefore, they matter to us

(Luke 5:30,32; Luke 15) Includes the concepts of relational evangelism and evangelism as a process.

4. Fully devoted followers are committed to continuous life change

(Philippians 1:6) Includes the concepts of small groups and accountability.

5. Authenticity is critical to spiritual and relational growth

(Ephesians 4:25,26,32) Includes the concepts of truth-telling, biblical conflict resolution and vulnerability.

6. The Church is culturally relevant

(1 Corinthians 9:19-23) Includes the concepts of using the arts in church services and facility issues.

7. All that we do is to honour God

(Colossians 3:17; Malachi 1:6-14) Includes the concepts of evaluation (critical review) intensity and excellence.

8. The Church is to be led by leaders

(Romans 12:6,8; Acts 6:2-5; Ezekiel 34:1-10) Includes the concepts of empowerment, servanthood, strategic focus and intent.

The issue of the values that we believe leading to the action we take is an important and welcome emphasis. As many biblical expositors have noted, the word 'therefore', used as a conjunction in the New Testament linking belief and behaviour, is of great significance. As Christians we want to allow the beliefs we hold shape the way we behave as individuals and as a Church. Maybe some of us need to sit down and review what values we believe in and how they impact our strategies.

The Community Charge

The emphasis given in Willow Creek's theology to the importance of the Church has brought increasingly the realisation that the Church is called to be a community. In a breathtakingly good session, repeated at current Leadership Conferences at Willow Creek, Dr Gilbert Bilzekian speaks about 'reclaiming biblical community'. It is a reminder that Willow Creek is a Community Church—a church where members are trying to allow Christ to make a difference to their relationships, their attitudes, their morality and their lifestyle.

The notion that Christ has freely accepted us means that the new community of God's people should be equally accepting of others. Where disharmony occurs in the church, Matthew 18:15-17 is taught as a realistic and practical way of sorting things out. It is surely not without significance that Church Leadership Conferences at Willow Creek begin with some Bible study on Acts 2:42-47 and end with a session on 'Reclaiming Biblical Community'.

This emphasis on community is, I think, especially important in the kind of society in which many of us find ourselves today. In a world where broken relationships increasingly play a part and where a lot of people feel damaged and rejected, a community of acceptance seems to hold real and potential significance. It is a sad reflection on many churches that such acceptance seems hard to find. Friends of mine have told me that they find more acceptance in public houses than they do in their, albeit irregular, visits to church.

Is there anyone out there?

This book is for those who feel a flicker of both challenge and excitement when they hear that 90% of the people of the UK are never in church. It's for those who are ready to make some kind of commitment to the unchurched people for whom Jesus Christ died. To think of such a commitment is both scary and invigorating. I think it means that our churches may need to change and start a new journey into unknown territory. This journey will require faith and courage, humility and patience, imagination and persistence, but I firmly believe it will be worth it. For we journey with the sure knowledge that God goes with us.

Travel well!

Note

1. *Starting a Seeker-sensitive Service*, Ed Dobson, Scripture Press (1994), p. 87.

APPENDIX I

How Can We Become More Seeker-Sensitive?

1. How relevant is our church building?
   - feel?
   - cultural backdrop?

2. How accessible is our worship?
   - books
   - music
   - language
   - posture
   - dress

3. What do we mean by 'we are a welcoming church'?
   - everyone's self-perception
   - importance of anonymity

4. What do people do with their children?
   - importance of good child care

5. How will they discover what to do with the children?

6. What do people do if they need a lavatory?

7. How user friendly are we to the disabled?

152 Reaching the Unchurched

8. What would a newcomer get from the sermon?

9. How relevant is your church to young people?

10. What is the attitude of your members to newcomers?

APPENDIX II

Questionnaire

1. Do you regularly attend a church?
   ☐ Yes   ☐ No

   How often?
   ☐ Weekly   ☐ Monthly   ☐ Festivals

If YES to Question 1

2. Which church do you attend?
   ☐ C of England   ☐ Methodist   ☐ Baptist
   ☐ Free church   ☐ Roman Catholic
   ☐ Other

3. Choose one or more of the following words which best describe your church.
   ☐ Caring   ☐ Friendly   ☐ Happy
   ☐ Traditional   ☐ Modern   ☐ Unfriendly
   ☐ Other

4. Choose one or more of the following words to describe your services.
   ☐ Boring   ☐ Moving   ☐ Traditional
   ☐ Modern   ☐ Complicated   ☐ Too long
   ☐ Other

What first attracted you to the church you attend?

_____

_____

If NO to Question 1

5. Choose one or more of the following words which best describe your perceptions of the church.
   - [ ] Boring
   - [ ] Irrelevant
   - [ ] Traditional
   - [ ] Modern
   - [ ] Unapproachable
   - [ ] Excellent
   - [ ] OK if you're a member
   - [ ] Other

6. Which of the following words would best describe any sermons you have heard?
   - [ ] Boring
   - [ ] Challenging
   - [ ] Interesting
   - [ ] Unintelligible
   - [ ] Irrelevant
   - [ ] Too long
   - [ ] Other

7. What about church music?
   - [ ] Too traditional
   - [ ] Too modern
   - [ ] Not what I like
   - [ ] Good
   - [ ] Poor quality
   - [ ] Too loud
   - [ ] Other

8. What do you enjoy most about Sundays?
   - [ ] Time to spend with family
   - [ ] A long lie in
   - [ ] Family day
   - [ ] Recreation
   - [ ] Free from a busy time-table

9. Given your answer to the last question, do you think it is sensible for church to be held on a Sunday?
   - [ ] Yes
   - [ ] No

   If 'No' could you give guidance as to a better time?

   Day _____ Time _____

10. If you wanted to know more about the Christian Faith, which of the following would you do?
    - [ ] Go to church
    - [ ] Ask the vicar
    - [ ] Buy a book
    - [ ] Ask Jehovah's Witnesses
    - [ ] Talk to a Christian friend
    - [ ] Other

Questionnaire

11. If a small group of people who all wished to know more about the Christian Faith, were meeting together, would this be helpful?
    ☐ Yes   ☐ No

12. If you had a crisis, in your life, would it occur to you to approach the Church?
    ☐ Yes   ☐ No

13. How do 'traditional' Church buildings make you feel?
    ☐ Welcome   ☐ Uneasy   ☐ Judged
    ☐ Overawed   ☐ Other